# AWAKEN THE GURU IN YOU

TRISH OTTONE

Copyright © 2020 Trish Ottone

All rights reserved. No part of this publication may be reproduced, distributed or transmitted in any form or by any means without permission of the publisher, except in the case of brief quotations referencing the body of work and in accordance with copyright law.

ISBN: 978-1-913479-62-6 (paperback)
ISBN: 978-1-913479-63-3 (ebook)

www.thatguyshouse.com

# IN PRAISE OF...

*"Awaken the Guru in You* is a fantastic guide on how to connect with and develop your intuition, how to navigate life, and most importantly, how to trust yourself - a must read!" – Emma Mumford, Author of *Spiritual Queen* and *Positively Wealthy*.

"Trish is a down-to-earth person with amazing intuitive gifts who consistently provides useful and insightful information that is both spiritual and practical at the same time. I am sure her new book will not disappoint!" – Belinda Stronach, Canadian corporate business leader and philanthropist.

"Trish Ottone is an extraordinary medium and intuitive advisor. Every time I have a session, she consistently amazes me with her accuracy, and I have benefitted greatly from her guidance. I highly recommend Trish as a fine-tuned instrument, who skillfully serves as a connection between her clients and the vast realms of universal knowledge." - Michael Gregory, Psychotherapist.

"I had no idea that I had a Guru inside me to guide me in my everyday life! But after reading this book, I love being able to tap into my own self and get the answers I've always struggled with. The self-discovery techniques she shares in this book are easy to follow and they work. Thanks, Trish! I am forever changed." - Elizabeth Campbell, Marketing & Communications Professional.

"Thanks to Trish's introduction, practical teaching, and energetic enlightenment, my self-image has done a 180-degree turn. Trish is a natural leader, and I consider myself a very fortunate individual because she walked into my life. Today, I too can be a beacon of light for the people whom I care for in my life." - Sue Paolucci, Civil Servant.

"Trish is an insightful, highly-skilled holistic practitioner. Her incredible gift of intuition for others provides an opportunity for healing, assurance of the present, and clarity for the future. I'd highly recommend her to anyone." - Susan Baker B.Sc., B.Ed., RHN.

*To my friends, family, peers, and all who have been a witness to my life. I recognize that I would not be who I am without having known all of you, and it is with the deepest gratitude I dedicate this book to all of you.*

# CONTENTS

INTRODUCTION ................................................................ ix

1. DISCOVERING THE GURU IN YOU ......................... 1

2. IGNITE THE GURU IN YOU ....................................... 19

3. EDUCATE THE GURU IN YOU .................................. 37

4. KNOW THE GURU IN YOU ........................................ 57

5. ESTABLISH THE GURU IN YOU ............................... 73

6. CULTIVATE THE GURU IN YOU .............................. 89

7. FINE-TUNE THE GURU IN YOU .............................. 111

8. INTEGRATING THE GURU IN YOU ....................... 127

9. EXPAND THE GURU IN YOU ................................... 147

10. DEEPEN THE GURU IN YOU .................................. 161

11. LOVE THE GURU IN YOU ....................................... 181

12. LIVE AS THE GURU IN YOU .................................. 201

RECOMMENDED READING ........................................ 218

ABOUT THE AUTHOR .................................................. 219

Awaken the Guru in You

# INTRODUCTION

x

# INTRODUCTION

What if I told you that you already possess what it takes to turn your life experience from ordinary to extraordinary? That you already possess the most amazing secret intelligence system than can totally turn your world around and make you your happiest, healthiest, most successful self. That it would not cost a thing other than some of your time and some attention. Would that sound like something you might be interested in?

You may be thinking, too good to be true. I promise you it is not. I am speaking of course of your *intuition*. Can you imagine having a deep confident knowing that guides your every decision in the right direction? Wouldn't navigating life become so much simpler if you had access to that kind of insight? The great news is you do! You were born with it, have always had it, and just need to learn how to make the most of it. Once you begin to know yourself deeper, you will begin to ignite your intuition and awaken *the guru in you*. This book shows you how to hone and develop that internal guidance system. Your intuition will lead you to amazing wisdom and insight that will help you make awesome improvements to your life and bring you into closer alignment with your true self.

I have worked as a psychic and medium for many years but even for me, it all began with developing my intuition. That is the one thing that led to me making the many changes and choices that have made me into the happy, healthy person I am today. So how do you do this then? This, as they say, is the million-dollar question. Step by step, one foot at a time, with self-love and compassion, and with dedicated consistency of action and behaviour.

There really is no quick fix but I can promise you that you are worth the effort and will reap many rewards if you love yourself enough to give yourself a chance to shine and develop your intuitive muscle. It's easier and more natural than you would ever think. Remember, you already have what it takes!

Still sounding too easy? Alright, here is the truth. Yes, there is some work involved. I would even say this will take a bit of bravery and perhaps even some spiritual metal. It is something that is at times equally as challenging as it is rewarding. You will have to be open to getting to know yourself at a very deep and intimate level, through the shadow and the light. You will have to get down and dirty with your "stuff" and wade about in your psychological and emotional crap a bit, but that is something we all must do at some point anyway. I promise you that with some dedicated effort and a whole lot of self-love and honesty, you will soon be moving through your life in new and wonderful ways. Life will seem so much less challenging and you won't ever be on an emotional roller coaster again.

I believe that we are all connected to and created from a Divine source, and that we have that same divinity with in us. I think that most of us are no longer working within paradigms and belief systems that support our divine design, and therefore we tend to experience all sorts of imbalances in our lives on physical, mental, emotional, and spiritual levels. We are out of touch with our own divine natures.

I believe that your intuition is the thread that can weave that divinity back into your awareness. It is something that helps us remember and strengthen our connection to our divinity. When you work to *remember who you truly are,* you tell the Universe that you are ready to re-embrace your Divine self and your true-life path with an unparalleled authenticity. I believe that we truly are spiritual beings on a human journey and that the two parts are inseparable. Reconciling these two parts into a harmonious union is, I believe, the key to a happy, peaceful, and healthy life. When this happens, life becomes less of a struggle and more of a joy to witness as it unfolds before your eyes.

This does not mean that there aren't hard decisions to make, or hard work to do. Often when we are doing something good for ourselves it doesn't actually "feel" good, or even comfortable, while we are in the middle of it. There are always challenges in life. After the work though, when a new vision appears from within, a new perspective and a new way of walking through this world, life becomes good, even great, and sometimes amazing. Life becomes a series of experiences that take you deeper into your true self and help to manifest even greater things and greater joy. That is when life gets very exciting!

Living more intuitively will help you become able to consciously co-create with the Universe and manifest true abundance to the degree that you have always wanted to but have been afraid to imagine for yourself. It will feel like unfamiliar territory a lot of the time and will perhaps be more work than you signed up for. The trade-off however is so worth it. Liberation from worry, struggle, and disharmony. Peace and joy in everyday life. Imagine a life with mostly good days, and one where the bad days barely impact you. I am living proof that it is possible. I somehow stumbled my way to happiness, and I want to share the things that I have learned along the way to help you experience all that too. If I can do it, anyone can.

I urge you to love yourself enough to awaken the Guru in you. Do this work and live life in a way you have never imagined. You have nothing to lose and everything to gain. If you have picked up this book, then something is already at work inside you urging you forward. Already you have come to the realization that what has worked for you in the past in terms of managing your life is no longer really working, and that something needs to change for there to be positive forward movement.

Let yourself be the change. Learn to listen to that little voice inside and thus be guided by your inner Guru. If you do, you will never be led astray and will become happier and healthier than you have ever been. I guarantee you that the most happy, balanced, and successful people on the planet live this way. Each day, they operate from that place of intuitive knowing and alignment. They may call it "gut instinct" or any other number of names, but what it all boils down to is that they are energetically aligned with their true nature. They have learned to listen to that "little voice" inside with trust and follow up that with action. That is what makes the difference between living an ordinary life and living an extraordinary life, and the best part is that you already have all the equipment you need – it's built right in!

Time, effort, and practice is all it takes to *awaken the Guru in you.* This book offers guidance, but really it is all up to you. These are all things that I have applied to my own life, so they are tried and tested methods. You are worth it and will find this out, as I have done. Once you learn your divine lessons and apply them to your life, everything will begin to change for the better. You will never regret the investment you make in yourself.

When you make that commitment to yourself – to truly know yourself deeply and intimately with awareness, you will begin to manifest not only all that you want but all that is sitting in potential for you. That is some powerful stuff! If you start to listen to that "little voice" inside and stop overriding it with your ego, logical mind, or even lack of confidence, you will begin to discover the magic that is in all of us waiting to be unlocked.

Your inner voice is the seat of your intuition, of your soul. It is the direct link to Divine knowledge and inner wisdom. Let this voice be your inner compass, guiding and directing you. This is how to co-create with the Universe and to attract all the things that are truly meant for you to live a loving peaceful life full of abundance, contentment, and happiness.

Once you start to connect more deeply with yourself, you will begin to connect with your guides and angels and unlock incredible magical things in the Universe. It is the beginning of it all. It is my deepest desire that this book will help to assist in that amazing process of unfolding for you, so you can manifest your own deepest wishes and heartfelt desires. Remember, you are already awesome and have all the answers inside you. Use this book to teach yourself how to listen and hear what you want to know.

# 1. DISCOVERING THE GURU IN YOU

## 1. DISCOVERING THE GURU IN YOU

Is there a Guru in you? I can understand if you wonder or have doubts. We have all been plagued with self-doubt and uncertainty. We have all likely felt a bit lost and confused and maybe even wished we had our own crystal ball to help us with insights and advice. The thing is that you do have that crystal ball. The reality is psychic gifts are a normal human endowment. We are all intuitive and we can all develop our intuitive psychic muscle if we want to. We can choose to use it every day to help us with insight, advice, and guidance.

Does this sound familiar? It's decision time, and there is that *little voice* inside your head urging you to make a move in one direction, but then comes that secondary voice that says no, go the other way. Perhaps it's more logical, rational, and familiar. How often do you ignore or brush off that *little voice* inside your head? We have all been there. It's normal. It is natural to struggle with that inside voice until you learn to trust it.

Learning to trust can be a big learning curve. That inside voice, or your *little voice,* is your intuition speaking. It is trying to get through. Your ego, however, likes to be in charge and in control. So, it is a natural response to squelch that *little voice* until you learn to trust it. That lesson of *Divine Trust* is a big one! Usually it takes time to really evolve to the point where you have a strong trusting relationship with your intuitive voice. If you practice though, you will get to a place where it speaks louder than the mental, logical, ego voice does.

Great wisdom is available to you today. Right now! By you, from you, for you. Your soul is speaking to you right now and it does so every day. Close your eyes just for a moment. Put your hands on your heart. Just do it. Listen as you feel your heart thumping. Listen with your feeling mind and not your thinking mind. There is a message there for you right now. Breathe in, be still and listen. It will happen and it's just the beginning.

I am not a crazy person. Often, we tend to equate intuitive and psychic ideas as scary, weird and even wrong – oh yes, we judge! The fact is that in many other cultures these abilities are not only normal but are often honoured. We all have spiritual gifts and we can all cultivate them into a beautiful, wonderful useful tools that guide us and assist us in our lives. The fact is simply that intuitive ability is our human birthright and more simply, it is part of our built-in defense mechanism. There is a physiological and anatomical response to intuitive ability that is undeniable.

Our intuition is an inherent silent language we all have that utilizes all our sensory elements (physical, mental, emotional, and spiritual) to speak to us. For example, when you get into a situation that you may need to be cautious about and you have a physical experience – like the hairs on your arm standing up or you get tingles or shivers – this lets you know mentally that something is up, which emotionally signals you to be on guard.

This physical feeling came from an "energy" that seemed outside yourself, yet you felt it connected to you on a deep internal level.

## 1. DISCOVERING THE GURU IN YOU

You did not have any prior rational or logical details about the situation, but intuitively you knew. Intuition is the name for this process. Sometimes we just know things. I would go so far as saying most of the time we know lots, but we have not been taught to make the most of it.

You may be wondering just what we need our intuition for? I mean what is the benefit, right? I always compare it to using a sharp pencil versus a dull one or trying to cut a roast with a dull knife versus a sharp one. We all know how much easier and more pleasurable everything is when you are using the right tool for the job. Working with your intuition is the same in that the sharper your intuition is, the better compass it becomes in helping you successfully navigate every aspect of your life. Wouldn't you want a tool like that? You already have it and can choose to develop it. Just like that.

Let's face it, you have already experienced your intuition. Even if you did not recognize it as that at the time, you have felt those inner nudges or knowing. You have heard and felt those inner impulses to do something or act in a certain way. Everyone has. Try and remember for yourself a time when you experienced that and listened. Now think of a time when you experienced that and did not listen. Think about how that did or did not work out for you. So, what happens when you ignore your intuitive promptings? When you ignore your intuition?

Generally, we are not encouraged to tune into our intuition. From early childhood, we are taught to follow and listen to external direction and wisdom (everything from parents and teachers to religious figures, politicians, television marketing, and advertising). So, from an early age, we are desensitized to developing a strong relationship with our intuitive gifts.

People ignore their intuitive vibes because they mentally talk themselves out of listening to *that little voice*. But when you do this, you stagnate the whole process. How does it feel when someone ignores you? How about when they ignore you time after time after time? You feel like giving up on them, right? It feels impossible to have a positive and productive relationship with someone who is constantly ignoring you. It's like they are telling you they don't care, trust or want you. When you ignore your intuition, it is the exact same. If you want it to work for you, you must pay attention to it. You must create a relationship with it. It is like every other relationship, it's a two-way street. You give, you get.

It's hard to face the truth in life, even when deep down you know what that truth is. For example, you may have been in a relationship or job that intuitively you knew was not healthy for you, but you mentally rationalized it because that is what worked for you on an emotional level. You made excuses for people and things because your heart wanted it, so your head accommodated that want, even though deep down something was telling you that it was not going to work.

You're not the only one that has been through this. Often, we ignore our intuition when it is telling us something that we do not want to hear. When this happens, it is simply fear taking control. Mastering your intuition means that you come to trust your intuitive impulses completely. You trust your intuition to the extent that you can surrender to its direction and knowing, despite your fears and in spite of your ego trying to keep you in your comfort zone. It takes work to get to this place of trust, but it sure makes life a lot less complicated.

So how does it all work? If we view the intuition as a receptor for information, then the stronger it is, the better it will receive signals. The body acts as the antennae carrying the receptor, so the healthier and more balanced the body is, the stronger the antennae will be. It's like having excellent wi-fi or a strong internet connection. The better the connection, the faster and more effective the internet is. Likewise, the healthier and happier and more balanced you become on all levels (physical, mental, emotional, and spiritual) when your intuitive signals are coming through loud and clear.

To create the balance that keeps your signals strong, pay attention to everything from exercise and nutrition to sleeping well and having healthy relationships. Anything that helps you connect with yourself and helps to cultivate your balance and harmony will all be things that will help your intuition develop. I live intuitively every day in pretty much every way. Frankly, I cannot imagine my life without that connection. I defer most decisions to my intuition, even down to the food I eat. For me, using my intuition is just like using my mind or breathing. It is a deep natural part of who and what I am. It is something that I rely on for not just my balance and happiness, but for my profession. I value it more than any other tool I own and am grateful every day for my connection. Because of this, I also do everything in my power to take care to do the right things in my life to keep that relationship nurtured and at its best.

I am often asked by clients, and by people in general, for advice on developing intuition. Aside from all the knowledge and techniques in this book, many things that help nurture happiness, calm, and balance will help in developing your intuitive muscle. Things like walking in nature, meditation, prayer, contemplation, yoga, proper sleep, good nutrition, and lots of water. Not only are these things great for health and stress management but they all help you to connect with yourself, and your soul essence. The better you know yourself, the easier it will be to cultivate your intuitive and spiritual gifts. The deeper you become aware of yourself, the deeper you will cultivate a relationship with your intuitive self and all the by-products that come with that.

I expect that you are feeling intuitive impulses in your life now or you wouldn't be reading this book. That *little voice* that speaks to you sometimes is your intuitive nerve saying, "Hello friend, here I am. Please let's have a chat and get to know one another. I am here to help you." Going forward, please do your best to listen. Do your best to take direction and to follow those impulses with actions. This will help you build that relationship and it will be so wonderful, you will wonder what took you so long to start listening. Pretty soon you will be having all kinds of conversations with yourself. It's a good thing.

Just remember that connecting to your intuition is the most natural and normal thing in the world, even if sometimes other people may question it. For example, successful people in business get a "gut feeling" and they are rewarded; a mother has a hunch and it is all good because it is accepted that mother's intuition is an actual thing; but if a co-worker has an urge to ask you to drive home a different way or they feel they should check in with their doctor, they can be labeled a weirdo (and yes, it has happened to me). It is time to get perspective, to get a grip, and to begin honouring and honing your own intuitive muscle to make a positive difference in your own life and in those around you.

Given that I work as a medium, people are always curious about my past. How did I get to be the person they have come to visit for a reading or healing? Like most people's lives, my journey to today was not a straight path. We all have a story to tell, a story that has shaped who we have become. I am no different and truly I do not think that there is anything special about me or my journey. Perhaps it is a less common experience, but no more special than anyone else's path.

I will say however, that along the way I was lucky enough to have recognized where my personal challenges led to insight. I have been able to identify these insights and how they have helped me to develop. I view them as a series of Divine lessons. Perhaps you also have challenges that you learned from and can relate to this. If you have never thought of your own challenges as a type of *Divine lesson*, it may be a new perspective that could help deepen your understanding of your own experiences.

## **A Story Of Divine Surrender**

Upon reflection I would say that the single most important thing that stands out in my mind about being different compared to other people, is that I have always seemed have a spiritual connection to and an awareness of what God is to me. Perhaps others have too, and I am just not aware of it. It has never really been a topic of discussion for people around me. I only know that from my very first memory, I have always known, believed, and trusted in this larger force outside of myself that I have always felt connected to. I am so very grateful for this and for never knowing or feeling a disconnection from that force.

It is because of this connection that I have always had what some would call faith. From that faith comes a certainty and knowing of belonging and of love. This has always helped me to access an inner strength and knowing that regardless of what I am experiencing, I will be taken care of.

I recognize this as a powerful gift, especially as I have encountered so many people who struggle with it. It is a gift however that does not come without its challenges. Having such a strong inherent belief in something that most people question or dismiss can get tricky. Sometimes it makes you stand out in ways that are difficult to navigate on a human emotional level. Sometimes it comes with harsh judgement, with isolation and with ridicule. Often it comes with knowing there is a higher road to take that most people do not see or recognize and one you are rarely acknowledged for nor ever thanked. Sometimes it can feel as if your knowing and your faith works against you. But this is never the case and if this is something you have experienced, be assured that those feelings soon pass and will be replaced by the comfort of knowing that ultimate love that resides with faith.

Another gift that I have full awareness of is that I was blessed with wonderful parents. I know how pivotal this is in the creation and foundation of one's life. God bless my parents because even though they often did not understand some of my choices and actions, they believed in who I was as a person, in my goodness. For this, I will be eternally grateful.

As an example, when I was three years old, my mother took me to see Santa Clause at the local shopping centre. Like many young children, I was mortified and stuck by fear at the deep voice, the ho-ho-ho, and the robust man in the red suit. Calming me my mother asked, "If you don't want to see Santa, what do you want?" Unlike many children, I replied that I wanted to go to the manger to be with baby Jesus because he was all alone. I guess you could say I have always been a bit different.

Certainly, I have always been very spiritually inclined and had an interest in world religions and theology. And yes, as a Roman Catholic teenager, I danced briefly with the idea of becoming a nun, because well, when you are a spiritually inclined person

## 1. DISCOVERING THE GURU IN YOU

and Catholicism is all you have been exposed to, you think being a nun is the natural thing to do. Turns out it was not the right spiritual path for me.

The path from there to spirit communication and full time medium started out pretty much as a normal Canadian childhood experience with a few surprising things along the way. I can assure that in no way did I ever think I would be doing what I do for a living. It was not even on my radar in any capacity. The first time I ever heard the word psychic, I was already in my early twenties. A friend asked me to go with her to a psychic reading that she had booked. "What is that?" I asked. "A lady is going to tell me my future," she said. "Oh, OK," I responded. I was always up for a road trip. This was probably the best first psychic exposure I could have asked for. This psychic lived on the edge of a lake in a chocolate box setting, was Danish in nationality, had a dog named Zen, and was a student of Paramahansa Yogananda (an Indian Monk who wrote *Autobiography of a Yogi*). Basically, not really *woo woo*, very calm and down to earth.

Since I had no interest in having a "reading" done, I browsed her bookshelves as she proceeded to do a tarot card reading for my friend. As a passing thought, I found it interesting that we had quite a lot of the same books. Remember I was OK with being a spiritual person. At this time, I was in college working towards a certification in marketing and advertising having just completed several years working towards a degree in political science. You can imagine my response when I heard her tell my friend that I was like her and I was going to do readings for people just like she did. I thought she was off her trolley. As far as I was concerned, I was going into corporate marketing, thank you very much. I was determined in that.

I am sure that the Universe, God, and all the Angels and Guides had quite a good chuckle at my expense that day. Personally, in response, I dug my heels in and refused to even think about it all. That psychic business was not for me and was not part of my plan. Later that year in college, I befriended a few girls that were a lot of fun. They were all what I lovingly call "psychic-aholics". They spent a good bit of time on the weekends going all over the city getting psychic readings. They had way more money than I did so I just went along for the ride and for the fun. It was all very entertaining. We went to psychic fairs and wellness shows and sketchy apartment buildings – it was quite an education! Little did I know that it was all experience to show me how not to work and how not to behave as a psychic and medium. The stories I could tell! But what I did learn was the psychic and spiritual business is like any other business. There are good honest integral people and there are less honest and less integral people. My advice would be to get referrals and trust your own instincts.

Along with these mishaps and adventures, several times I experienced what I had before. Readers and healers alike would look at me and say things like, "Oh, you have healing energy you should do Reiki." "What is reiki?" I would ask. "Oh, you have the gift. You are going to do this. Everywhere you go, people are going to know you and love you for what you do." "Thank you, yes, I have gifts in marketing and advertising, and I am going to the city to work," I would reply. This went on for a few years. It is true what they say, what is for you will not pass you by. Despite my resistance, things caught up with me, and I began to realize for the first time the meaning of Divine surrender.

On one of my excursions, I walked into a New Age bookstore where my friends had organized readings. Looking back, this was a pivotal day in my life for a few specific reasons. By this time, I was working in marketing and involved in my first serious

## 1. DISCOVERING THE GURU IN YOU

romantic relationship. I was 28 years old and had been learning about energy work through reading books and had explored tarot cards a little bit. I had been meditating since I was 17 and exploring my spiritual path in various ways. Nothing major, just general interest stuff. I was always interested in all kinds of spirituality. This day two significant things happened that would set me on a new course for life, though it would take several years still before I would understand it all.

As I walked into the store, I had what could be termed a paranormal experience of sorts. It was as if someone stood right in front of me blocking my path and put their hand to my cheek turning my face to look at a rack of books. As this occurred, I heard a loud swoosh sound. Yes, I felt the hand and heard the sound. Now by this time in my personal spiritual development, I had already been a meditator for several years and I had already developed an awareness of spirit guides. All of this was OK by me. It did not mean to me that I was psychic in any way and certainly not a medium. I had never heard of that before, the career path called "medium". But things were about to change forever.

As my head turned, my eyes were automatically drawn to a particular book in a rack of books. This rack was stacked with all the same book on it and one book in the centre of the rack was reversed and it had the author's picture on it. My eyes went directly to hers in such a manner that I knew I was being given the message to buy that book. I was along my path far enough at this point to recognize the sign. I just figured it was a message from my guides and so I bought the book. This was the first significant thing that day that forever changed my life.

Having bought the book, I awaited my turn. This day I was actually going to get a reading myself. I walked into the room and was met by a very intense and enthusiastic young woman similar in age to me who threw herself up out of her chair and embraced me, telling me she thought I was the reason she had moved to Canada (aside from her husband). I was polite. I just thought that she was a little intense.

She stepped back, collected herself, and introduced herself and began my reading using tarot cards. Very early into the reading she gave me a look. Sarcastically she said, "So, you're pretty intuitive huh?" I thought, here we go again. I said, "Yes, people have said that I am psychic, but I really don't take it too seriously." Then she launched an attack. "Well, it's easier not to isn't it? Then you don't have to take any responsibility for anything do you?" and so forth. This went on for what seemed a very long time. I thought to myself, "Really, I am paying for this?"

To be honest, she was so over the top it shocked me, and I do not shock easily. What shocked me most however was that I realized that she was right. I had been called out in such an outrageous way that I could not deny it any longer. I could not justify putting my head in the sand and hiding from what was obviously my destiny. In that moment, I experienced Divine surrender and my true path in life began to unfold before me. My response was to laugh out loud. "You're pretty intense" I said to her. "I am from New York," she said. "Ah," I replied, and that was that. Within a week, I was attending her tarot class and after the third class, she just asked me to co-teach it with her because I was a natural. Within a few more weeks, she had booked me to do reading parties with her and we were making plans to co-facilitate workshops, classes, and seminars.

Off I went home with the book that had called to me, and I really did not look at it for a couple of months. During the week, I was a marketing person, and, on the weekends, I was a psychic.

## 1. DISCOVERING THE GURU IN YOU

That lasted for about six months. During that time, I had also been developing a meditation course and so I diligently worked away on my material, continuing to pursue my own spiritual development, cultivating my gifts, and honing my psychic abilities.

Over this time frame, I finally began to read the book I had purchased which essentially told the life story of, you guessed it, a medium.

It began when this woman was only four years of age and took her life right up to that present day. In it she described the unfolding of her life as a medium. She described many experiences that I found myself able to relate to and some that I had exactly experienced myself over my life. After the sixth time I related to an exact occurrence in her life, I shut the book. I was only halfway through reading it and I was quietly freaking out. It seems I was OK with being a psychic, but I was not at all comfortable connecting to dead people. I shelved the book.

For the next six months, I carried on in the same fashion and had many life altering experiences happen. This period of my life was very much an emotional rollercoaster fraught with so many personal and professional challenges.

At the end of this six months, I experienced my second Divine surrender. I finally surrendered to the fact I was a medium, like it or not. At the end of the day, I decided that if this was what God wanted me to be then who was I to stand in the way of that. Resisting certainly was not getting me anywhere, so I picked up the book and finished it and have been working as a medium ever since.

As you work to develop your intuitive skills and gifts, you will learn that the very act of doing so will lead you down a somewhat spiritual path. This is something that you need to get comfortable with. Personal growth, increased awareness, and the evolution of yourself in the world around you, are all interconnected. One naturally leads to the other. Perhaps this is the Universe's way of ensuring some quality control? I only know that it is impossible to develop intuitively without really knowing yourself on deep levels. I also accept that ultimately the intuitive path and the spiritual path become one path.

Not everyone has a desire to develop psychic or mediumship skills, but everyone will benefit from cultivating their intuition. Having spiritual path or practice, whatever that is to you, will only add to your life. That is the anchor that will help you to work through life in a balanced way. As you deepen your relationship with yourself you will awaken spiritually and intuitively, and as that occurs you will begin to feel more connected to the world around you and to the Universe.

Intuitive ability is an innate sense and skill all of us have. Developing this skill is completely under your own control. Choosing to develop the senses and associated skills will help you to live a richer, fuller life. However, the same principles apply here as with anything else, you get what you give.

## **Intuitive Training Tip #1 - Self-Discovery Technique**

Spend some time contemplating your past. Think back as far as you can and try to identify some different times in your life where your intuition may have influenced the decisions that you took, even if you did not recognize that it was your intuition working then. Perhaps there were times you paid attention and listened to it, and other times when you disregarded it. What were the outcomes? Are there any lessons that you can glean from those situations?

Try to map out the most significant experiences or decisions that you can think of. Perhaps make yourself a timeline from when you were very young to present day. What were the significant events in your life that you feel changed you in some way? Think about what you learned going through those experiences and where a Divine lesson might be present for you. How could you apply that lesson to a current situation or challenge in your life?

If you can identify a current challenge or situation connected to one of your Divine lessons, examine how you intuitively feel about it. This will help you to learn how you may be receiving and processing intuitive information. The more familiar you get with how your intuition registers and works with your thinking, the better and faster you will begin to work with it.

## **Quick Recap:**

You are intuitive and you have that ability right now. Developing your intuition will take some work on your part, but the benefits will far outreach the efforts required. As you develop your intuitive skills, you will start to navigate life's challenges with greater ease than before. You will experience some changes physically, mentally, emotionally, and spiritually, because your thoughts affect the *whole* person that you are, and the intuitive path and the spiritual path are connected. If you are dedicated and committed to doing some personal work and some practical practice, you will deepen your self-knowledge and thus your intuition.

# 2. IGNITE THE GURU IN YOU

## 2. IGNITE THE GURU IN YOU

Working as a psychic and medium for the past twenty-five years, I have watched with interest and been encouraged in the last decade to see there has been a massive growth in mainstream interest in psychic phenomena and intuitive development. There is real depth to these gifts that goes far beyond mere prediction and parlour tricks.

However, I know as well as you do that there will always be sceptics. Personally, I have long since left the nay-sayers behind and focused on listening to myself and on helping others in the ways I know how, through self-development and personal healing. We all have a desire and a right to live healthy happy lives. This comes with a price tag of truth and acceptance. Anyone willing to pay (invest) that price will know no limitations in their personal growth and happiness. If you are willing to do the work, you will reap the rewards. I feel however it is necessary to address a misconception. People seem to think that intuitives, psychics, clairvoyants, healers and so forth, know the future and can predict things. In reality, a psychic can sense and perceive probabilities in the energy that surrounds a person that he or she may not be able to perceive. The psychic gets his or her impression from the presentation of energy at a given moment as well as the receptiveness of their own energy, which is based on the health and balance of their receptor.

Things that a psychic may tell you are never set in stone. We all have a uniquely human characteristic known as *free will* and it is the most powerful quality that each of us possesses. The future is not a fixed entity – static and set. It is energy, more precisely it is potential energy in motion, and it is greatly affected by decisions made in any given moment. Once you begin to learn how to pay attention to how you truly respond to and process energy and information, you will become more in tune with yourself. Then your inherent intuitive abilities will move to the forefront. It is all about a level of conscious awareness and the application of the information that said awareness brings you. Once you develop a true and honest relationship with yourself, you will develop an iron clad intuitive ability that you can use every day to create the life you have always wanted to live. Remember though – relationships take work. There is no escaping that part.

As with everything else, there are certain rules or governing laws that exist when working with energy and vibration, and as you bring out your own intuitive gifts, these will become apparent to you. Practice enough and you will master your intuition. Work hard to develop your intuitive muscle and it will be strong and serve you well. Simple right? There really is no big secret here. It is all very practical. All that is required is a desire to tap into the inner knowing that you already possess and a will to push forward. What have you got to lose *really*?

As you make the decision to embark on developing your skills, be aware that this is not an all or nothing situation, it is a process. There is no need to buy hemp clothing, drink matcha tea, or learn a new language. Know that step-by-step is the way forward. Begin with small changes and take things one day at a time. Work to cultivate an inner stillness and make efforts toward increasing personal balance in your life. As you do this, a sense of that inner calm will naturally happen and become more consistent as you do the work. As you go along, this will lead to a deeper connection with your intuition.

Let's face it. Most of us have a history that has on some level made us feel that we are unworthy of this or that. *Enough.* Enough of that crap. The past is done. We have no input on that anymore. Let it go and become responsible for today. You choose how to move forward from this moment on. You are a wonderful powerful being who can do great things. You were designed to do just that!

Don't get me wrong. If you feel that part of responsible action is to heal old wounds, great. Do it. Get therapy. Talk to someone. Just do it, so you can get on with building a sound future and creating fulfillment, satisfaction, health, and happiness. Forget the drama. It's overrated and exhausting, not to mention energy sucking. It's time for fun. It's time for awe and laughter. It's time to feel lighter and happier.

My life, and most specifically my path to being at one with the intuitive being that I am, has taught me a few certainties. I know with certainty that unfailing guidance is there for you. It is within you right now just waiting for you to access it and work with it. Identifying it is easy to do, just begin to pay attention. Really pay attention. To everything! Become an expert at recognizing subtleties and nuances. It will serve you so well. It will become like a secret weapon. It will become your superpower.

Sometimes it takes conflict of some kind such as emotional upheaval, heart storms, or a healing crisis to push us towards change. These things can push us to ask, "There has to be more to this. There has to be more to me." *There is.* There is so much more to you than you realize. Sometimes we need our Angels to take out the baseball bats and give us a thump before that insight makes its way up to our brain and our mental awareness. I know it has in my life!

There are two reasons that I am sharing the following story: Divine Faith and Divine Trust. I am sharing this to help ignite and encourage faith, rather than bring into question having it. I had my own healing crisis at a young age and through that ordeal, I feel my spiritual essence was really ignited. It seemed to trigger for me a deepening of my spiritual connections and an awakening of my intuitive self to new levels. It certainly began to teach me the importance of maintaining balance in life. Perhaps you have had an intense experience at some point in your life that has impacted your own spiritual ignition? Even if you do not feel that it was obviously intense to others, I bet that it deepened you in some way which has in turn impacted your life and maybe even your trust and faith.

## **A Story Of Divine Faith And Trust**

When I was seventeen years old, I was quite ill. I had developed a strange cough that became irritating to my father (thankfully!). After reams of tests resulted in no diagnosis, I was admitted to the hospital for a deep biopsy, one that required a hospital stay and a small surgery that I need to be knocked out for. No big deal I was told. I remember calling my mother that morning as they were prepping me and telling her I would see her in a couple of hours when I was back up in my room.

Nine hours later I was wheeled back into my room and from what I am told, I was barely recognizable to them. It seems that

## 2. IGNITE THE GURU IN YOU

I had had a cancerous tumour the size of a melon removed from behind my sternum that had begun to grow over my heart. They believed that they had removed it all and had it not been found, I would have certainly been dead in mere months.

I remember waking up in what would have been post-op and feeling like a tractor trailer truck was sitting on my chest crushing me. I remember trying to scream without success and managing to speak the word *pain*. Then I heard a nurse shout she's awake and a man in scrubs said, "Oh my God she is awake, get...." and that was it, I was out.

The next thing I recall was someone moving my feet and it was irritating as hell and I was really pissed off. I was angry. Clearly on some level I knew I had been violated in some way. To say the next few days were interesting is putting it mildly. I woke up with no less than twelve tubes in me. I was understandably grumpy even though I am lighthearted by nature. I was also forced to miss a Springsteen concert. It doesn't get much more unfair than that.

Prior to this I has been such a healthy athletic girl. I feel because of this, I bounced back quickly from such intense surgery. Within 48 hours, I had all of those tubes removed and was back to my perky self – still put out about the concert though. Also, I had had an amazing experience of sorts that had shown me the power of the mind. When it came time to remove some tubes that had been draining my lungs, I was already tired of being poked and prodded and needled. So, I declined to have any freezing while they removed those lung tubes. The tubes were sewn into my body and the procedure required that the stiches be cut, the tubes pulled out and then the skin re-stitched. I told them go ahead, I would just breathe through it. To this day I have no idea where that came from. I just felt a vibe and I went with it.

During the procedure, one of the nurses exclaimed, "Where did you learn how to do this?" She meant how did I know how to control the pain through breathing. I had no answer for her. I just knew that I could. I had faith that I could. I never once felt scared. I just knew that I wanted those foreign things out of my body and I just wanted to be left alone to heal and feel better.

As luck would have it, that whole episode took place at the beginning of my summer holidays from school. Mostly I remember sleeping, and I slept everywhere: inside in bed; on the couch; out in the garden; for hours and hours I slept. One time I woke to my mother shaking me. She said that she just wanted to make sure that I was alive! I slept for about seventeen hours a day. It was a strange time for me. Not because I had just gone through an intense surgery but more because of the isolation afterward. I was basically home alone a lot as my parents worked. That compounded by all of the sleeping left me feeling that I was kind of between worlds. My exhaustion was so complete that I would be reading or speaking and then just fall asleep and wake up hours later. At that time, we lived in the countryside and my friends did not really have access to me. Also, they did not quite know how to handle my illness I guess, and it was their summer holidays.

Through all of this, I never once felt lonely or sorry for myself because I had gotten ill. I just honestly did not think about it very much and kind of dealt with each day as it came. It was during this time that I began to meditate. I began to feel very connected to everything around me. It was like being alive on new levels. Everything felt different. The wind on my skin; the smell of grass freshly mowed; the buzzing of bees; the fragrance of lilacs on the breeze.

## 2. IGNITE THE GURU IN YOU

It sounds kind of silly, but it felt like all my senses had had their volume turned up. I did not think of it as anything specific. I just thought that because I was doing nothing but hanging out and napping outside a lot, I was just paying more attention than usual. Then one day I happened by a window and just outside it there were two hummingbird copulating. I stared and watched and in that very moment, I recognized the gift that I was being shown.

In my brain, in that instant, I realized that there was wonderous magic around us all the time, and that we only needed to pay attention to see it. As strange as it may sound, I felt very empowered by this. It gave me a deep understanding that though you may be experiencing something truly challenging or terrible, like getting cancer, there are still amazing things to experience, if you see past that terrible thing. I learned in an instant that perspective is everything and that what you choose to put your attention and focus to is what really can make a difference in your life. I learned that we all have a choice in how we experience our lives and all that we go through. Perspective is a choice and that is what can make all the difference in the world to your happiness. Think about it, have you been shown signs too that are subtly letting you know that you are on the right path or that you are being supported by the Universe? I bet if you begin to pay attention you will start to see them everywhere. They can really help to bring a new perspective to challenging situations.

For me it felt as if suddenly, I was standing in a ray of light and had just been shown one of the secrets of the world by a higher source. It made me realize how powerful we are, and how blessed we are if we choose to see the blessing and the gift that is life. I learned the lesson of everyday magic and it strengthened my faith that everything in life has a purpose, even the things that seem wrong or unfair or challenging. Pretty deep stuff for a 17-year-old.

A few weeks later I returned to school. It was my final year and I was really excited to be back in the groove with my friends and back to my life. On the third day of school, I returned home only to find out that I had been called to return to the hospital. "For how long?" I asked my mother. "They aren't sure," was her reply. I was shattered. I thought I had done so well staying so positive and I just wanted to be back on track and get on with my life.

It turned out that the tumour they had removed from me was not the only problem. I was admitted to the hospital once again and ended up remaining there for two full weeks for testing. I tried to stay positive, but I was really down. As much as I could, I remembered the hummingbirds and tried to change my perspective. It was hard being poked and prodded beyond what I thought was appropriate. I had every test you could imagine, and some of them were none to pleasant or easy. I was cut, stabbed, poked, you name it. Let's just say my spiritual mettle was being tested big time!

When you are stuck in a hospital, things get very small very quickly. Isolation in that kind of environment can seem to turn against you. It's very different from being alone at home with the company of your things, and of nature all around you. At the end of your day, you know family will arrive and things will feel OK once again. So, you make the most of little acquaintances. The chance to have a laugh or a giggle with someone becomes almost lifesaving. Watching a television program in the lounge brings the hope of escaping your situation for even the shortest of time and avails the chance to feel "normal" even for a little while. You begin to not care what show is on. Perspective again, right?

I was lucky enough to make a friend. I would run into this person and have a chat and a laugh. It was so nice to see a smiling face and have someone to connect with. I looked forward to seeing them, and it really brightened up my day, and theirs too. Slowly I began to feel more positive and chipper.

Then one day, I went to find my friend and her room was empty. There was no sign of her at all. It was like she had never been there at all. I went to inquire thinking perhaps she had gone home, lucky girl. I asked a nurse where my friend was. "Oh gone," she said. "Gone where?" I asked thinking maybe she had just been moved to another room. The nurse looked at me and said, "You know, gone." It turned out that my friend had died in the night and she was gone for good.

I cannot properly express the impact this had on me. It was a profound moment I will never forget. In that moment I had such a deep recognition of two things. Firstly, I was deeply aware of the frailty of life, of just how delicate life truly is. I felt this on an almost cellular level. It was so visceral and quite surreal. Secondly, and as deeply, I was awakened to the gift that is life. Truly, in an instant, I felt I had no business not embracing the gift of life even though paradoxically I was in the hospital with cancer. In that instant my illness was no longer relevant in any way because I was still breathing, still conscious, and as such still able to embrace the gift that is life itself. I had instant perspective. It was like a profound spiritual awakening in a way. I feel that experience has largely contributed to my positive nature and to my ability to keep perspective in spite of life's challenges.

The following day, my test results came back. It turned out that I had yet another type of cancer called Hodgkin's Disease. I would potentially always have it and right then, it was at a very serious level. I would need to have radiation therapy for several months and if I made it past a five-year "shadow period" of remission, then I would likely be OK and live a pretty normal life.

Well I can tell you that as I watched my mother struggle and try to be strong and positive for me, all I could think was how lucky I was to be alive and to still be sitting there in a hospital with my mother. I thought about my friend who was no longer alive and about those hummingbirds. I did not feel scared. I felt hopeful. I felt happy to know that I had potentially a normal life to live. I had been given more perspective and, in that moment, it was not lost on me how blessed I was to still be alive and to have people trying to help me and people who cared about me. I had faith that whatever was going to happen I would be OK because I was still here.

Eventually, the radiation treatment began. I will not pretend that it was anything but horrible. From start to end, horrible. This was back in the day when radiation was given to a person by having them lay underneath a big machine whereby, they were basically zapped for about 15 minutes with radiation. It is very different now, far gentler. This previous method caused my skin to burn after a few sessions. It was very uncomfortable, and it had a horrible smell to it. You just knew it was unnatural and wrong on some level.

However, radiation killed cancer cells and that was the point after all. I was scheduled to have more than 24 session in all. Fifteen on my neck and chest area and I think a dozen or so on my lower groin area. Hodgkin's Disease is cancer of the lymphatic system, so they had to cover all the major lymph areas. I was to be premedicated prior to all sessions to help deal with the effects and with nausea.

Believe it or not, my first session was scheduled on New Year's Eve. I am not sure if it was the excited air of the evening's celebration or the exhaustion of the festive season, but either way the nursing staff forgot to premedicate me. Since both

## 2. IGNITE THE GURU IN YOU

my parents worked. my poor older brother was given the task of taking me to the appointment. We were unaware of the premedicating and so naively thought that things had gone as they were meant to have.

It turns out, we had to pull over no less than nine or ten times before we got home so I could be sick. I have never been so ill in all my life. He practically had to carry me into the house. As I lay wretching on our kitchen floor, my head lolling about as I could not lift it, my mother was calling the clinic in pure panic to find out what was happening. The only thought in my head was that, in no uncertain terms, I could not go through this another twenty plus times. I knew intuitively on a soul level I could not do it. I literally thought I was going to die and that if I did live past this day then I would rather take my chances with the cancer than go through this again. We were all shell-shocked. That was when we found out that the premedication had not been given. We were told they were sorry and that it would not happen again. As I said, those were different times and there was no recourse for us. My next appointment was in two days.

As you can imagine, my parents both accompanied me to my next appointment. Prior to that, after I had recovered some of my strength, I thought I literally must have the worst luck on the planet. Again, I thought about the hummingbirds and about my friend in the hospital who did not come out. I thought about sitting outside in the summer and how magical all those connections were. Deep down I knew that it was not my time to die and so I surrendered to the fact that I had to endure this treatment and I trusted that there were reasons for all of this even if I did not know what they were.

Over the next several months, I endured radiation therapy and all that came with it. Naturally, my parents wanted me to stay home from school through all of it. I was not having that. It was bad enough I had to go through it all, but I did not want to lose my year as well. It was a big year, my graduating year. I did not want to get left behind. I can be a savvy negotiator and I am sure that they could see how much it meant to me. I needed something to hang onto and to look forward to that would make me feel like a normal 17-year-old through all of it. So, throughout my radiation therapy, I stayed in school, studied, and attended classes when I was well enough to. I missed a lot of time, but I kept up with the work. It was all very strange. Once again, I became very isolated in ways. I was with my friends when I was at school and when I was able to socialize on weekends. Things were just not the same though.

Before long, I began to feel completely emotionally isolated. Most people treated me the same, but I could always feel a weird undertone with my friends. They did not quite know how to interact with me. On my end, I began to have serious trouble relating to them. The things that mattered to them seemed so frivolous and shallow to me. It made things very tough emotionally for me. My family was all freaked out with my illness and they became different too.

It seemed like even though I was the one that had gone through everything, and was still going through everything, that I was the one being punished with isolation. I had to dig deep, and I can tell you that soon even the hummingbirds just weren't cutting it anymore. That was when I really turned toward my spiritual life. I delved into meditation and all things connected. I found myself a whole new world and though it likely moved me into further isolation and non-relatability to my peers in some ways, it also brought profound satisfaction, excitement, and tremendous comfort.

## 2. IGNITE THE GURU IN YOU

I learned how *very not alone* I was. I began to trust in huge ways the new path I found myself on. Little by little, the other things did not bother me so much and while I still felt isolated in ways from my peers and my family, I knew that it was not personal. It was only because I had experienced things they had not. It helped me reconcile it all and helped me to keep my focus on my healing and on my spiritual and personal growth.

Difficult times tend to make us search for something to make things better. Truly better, not just a quick fix. Whether or not people are comfortable with the words, what they are reaching for at times like this is *spiritual guidance*. I know that I found this to be true for me. When I felt the lowest in my life, I was forced to reach out in new ways that expanded my openness to all things, including those connected to spirituality. I read everything I could get my hands on. My personal challenges helped to ignite my desire to be healthy and happy, and I found those means through exploring my spirituality. As I did the self-exploration and personal work required to heal, I also learned how truly powerful and intuitive I was. This was the gift of my illness.

I read self-improvement books, books on energy healing, took yoga classes, walked in nature, explored oracle cards, and kept up with my meditation. These things and more can work for you in the same way. Once you strive to unite your physical, mental, emotional, and spiritual self, you will find ways to improve your life and heighten your own intuitiveness. Often the way is found through the vehicle of something on the spiritual spectrum.

Allow yourself to be ignited. Think about anything you feel drawn to that might be under that enormous spiritual umbrella that is out there. Go for a walk in your favorite bookstore and check out the self-help and spirituality sections. Have a look through YouTube and see if there are any vloggers that may appeal to you. Listen to a new podcast that is self-help or Law of Attraction oriented. Really anything that speaks to you in a positive way is the place to begin. The point is just to begin. Intuitively pick something you feel drawn to and just start. Don't be surprised to find that one thing will lead you to the next thing.

It is also perfectly normal at times to feel unsure or uncertain, so if you are feeling that way, know that it is OK! As you practice and develop intuitively you will learn to discern those feelings of uncertainty. Sometimes they are a sign of simple growth, usually when you are stepping out of your comfort zone in some way. Other times they may be a sign that something is not right for you and you are being flagged or warned to not continue on in a certain way. These trial and error periods are natural and important on your development journey as they help to hone your discernment skills.

## **Intuitive Training Tip # 2 – 3rd Eye Focusing Technique**

One of the key elements in developing your intuition is the ability to achieve a high and intense level of focus. Learning to develop and maintain your focus for extended periods of time is paramount to achieving greater depth and scope in your intuitive abilities. This exercise in concentration will assist in that development. Remember to be patient with yourself and build your practice time up slowly.

Read the following directions through entirely and practice as often as you are called to. The more you practice, the easier it will get and the stronger your control will become.

## 2. IGNITE THE GURU IN YOU

Light a candle and place it at a comfortable distance in front of you, at least 4 feet away.

Focus directly on the flame for approximately 2 minutes (you can blink – just be sure to keep your focus on the flame – not the candle)

Close your eyes and sit comfortably. You should see the flame appear in your *mind's eye,* like a visual inside your brain in the centre of your vision.

Hold the image of the flame in place for as long as you can. If it tries to move away, off to the side, control the image and bring it back to the centre of your vision. Make note of any interesting points such as the flame changing size or colour. Is it just the flame you see or is it the whole candle? Make a mental note of anything that strikes you as interesting.

When the image has finally and fully disappeared, open your eyes and journal your experience. Be sure to keep note of any interesting observations, thoughts, feelings, emotions, physical details, and so forth. Remember to write down the date so that you can track your progress. Practice this exercise often and notice how the length of time you can hold the image in your mind's eye before it fades or changes. As time goes on, you should be able to hold it for longer and longer periods of time. If at first you do not see a flame, do not get discouraged. Remember it is like the first day at the gym, it takes time to get those muscles in shape!

## **Quick Recap:**

Know that deepening your relationship with yourself is the key to health and happiness. As you do this you will likely want to explore your own spirituality in the process. Yes, there will always be sceptics, but learning to listen and trust yourself will always serve you best. Remember that things are never set in stone. You can change anything in your life that you want to. The energy you feel in and around you can always be changed. Know that you always have control. You choose how you move through the situations and challenges in your life. You control your perspective, and that perspective determines your experience.

We all have *free will* and that is the most powerful quality you possess. Paying attention to how you process and respond to energy and information will help nurture your intuitive abilities. This will help you deal with the situations in your life with more ease and awareness. As you develop and hone your intuition, you will begin to know and understand that solid unfailing guidance is within you *right now*. Most importantly remember that this is all a process, so be patient and kind with yourself along the way.

# 3. EDUCATE THE GURU IN YOU

## 3. EDUCATE THE GURU IN YOU

I believe learning to develop your intuition it is one of the best gifts you can give to yourself. The more time, energy, and effort you devote to your development, the more heightened your intuitive awareness and skills will become. It doesn't happen overnight, as I said it's really more like a process. It is important to keep in mind that we all develop at individual degrees and levels of ability, so think about being on a spectrum. Knowledge, skill, and ability are all very individual things, and our processes are also individual with numerous variables to consider such as background, cumulative experiences, age, and health for example. Always keep an eye to your own focus and try to avoid comparing yourself to others. That is merely an ego-driven mental action that will only create blocks for your own development.

There are exceptions to every rule, but what matters most is your own journey. I have met extremely gifted psychic people who it seems did not have to work too hard at all to experience psychic things. However, I have rarely met one who walked with life balance, had great health, possessed a humble ego, and just naturally had a keen discernment with an ability to understand the experiences they were having or the messages they were receiving. To be able to utilize your psychic gifts in a consistent and healthy way takes a steady and strong mind and a high level of emotional intelligence. These are things that can only be cultivated the old-fashioned way with commitment, dedicated hard work, and a lot of practice.

Now it is time for the fun stuff! It's time to start learning how to develop an awareness of the intuitive realm and honing the skills to work within that realm. In doing so, you will grow personally and spiritually, in every way. If you learn to navigate life better and reach your full potential health and happiness, you will have an impact on society at large and the positive ripples will continue to move out. If you do nothing with your intuitive skills but live a better life, everyone you connect with in any way will reap the benefits.

The intuitive path and the spiritual path are invariably connected. They both go hand-in-hand and the development of one without the other will not lead you to the potential you seek. Neither will happen to any real degree without discipline, consistency, and focused action. These are the essential components of development. While you may have some degree of natural ability, the fact remains the finessing of skills and talent is something that needs to be worked at.

The psychic energic realm, which is the realm of spirit, is very powerful and it comes with its own governing laws and rules. It must be understood, processed, valued, and above all respected. As you begin to study, work with, and know this realm, you will find it is far less mysterious and far more practical than you likely imagine.

Let's start by discussing the subtle realms. When we speak of the realm of spirit or of the psychic realm, we are simply

## 3. EDUCATE THE GURU IN YOU

discussing the realm of *subtle energies*. Essentially, these are the non-physical realms and layers of the universe. They are beyond the mundane tactile world and encompass what the human eye generally cannot see.

We are all beings of several layers, and most of these layers are made up of subtle energy bodies or energy fields. For example, you may have heard the term *auric field* or heard people refer to the *aura*. This refers to the energy layer that surrounds living things and some people can see the auric field around things and people. It looks a bit like a BBQ haze with various colours in it.

Our outer energy layers, or energy fields, are known as our *energy bodies*. We all have several of them and they ripple out, if you will, from your physical body. Imagine that you are enclosed by a circle of energy completely surrounding you, like you are in the middle of an egg. Now picture several other eggs surrounding that. This is how we all are constructed. Our outer layers of energy move out from our physical body. They include the Etheric body, the Emotional body, the Mental body, the Astral body, the Etheric Template body and finally the Causal body. All surrounding one another and all influencing one another. Together they make up your auric field.

Part of our functioning minds, our consciousness, as well as our senses, exist in the subtle realms all the time. This is what some people refer to as the sixth sense. The ability to sense things in the subtle realms. As a medium I am able to access information in these subtle realms and communicate with others who now exist only in the subtle realms.

These subtle realms, to some degree, dictate how we act in the physical realm, since all our senses exist on the subtle realms first. Our physical dense state is subservient to our subtle bodies and is the last place things manifest. This is how certain energy healing practitioners are able to sense dis-ease in an energetic body that has not manifested in the physical body yet as a disease or illness. This is also why sometimes you can *feel or sense* something that seems outside yourself. It is because you are feeling it with your energy body on the subtle realm before you feel it with your physical body on the physical realm.

The simple basics of science and energy tell us that all things are made up of matter, and all matter is made up of energy. When beginning the study of energy, these simple facts still apply and are the basis of all that you will learn. We then, as living organisms, are made up of energy and not just purely physical forms. We are electrochemical and electromagnetic beings made up of *energy fields* that maintain constant activity. Like all matter when broken down into molecules, we are made of pure energy. The physical form that you see as your human body is just energy appearing in a very dense and heavy form.

There are different types of energy and different energy fields. Each of these energies has its own identity. Each has its own consciousness, vibration, memory, and personality. Each field vibrates at its own individual and unique frequency. Have you ever noticed in life that sometimes you come across certain people, places, or things that for some unexplainable reason you know you just do not like or are immediately uncomfortable with? It could be someone that you've never met, and this could be a truly nice person but for some reason you want nothing to do with them.

What is happening is your personal vibration is just not a positive reciprocal of their vibration. Think of it like musical notes. Your vibration may be close to a C note on a certain scale and they may be an F or a G on a completely different scale. This works in reverse as well. How many of us have met someone and immediately felt good and comfortable in that person's presence? Immediately connected? You are both vibrationally at the same point, so you are like complementary notes and scales.

Your note or *vibration* is like your soul's fingerprint on the different fields by which you are identified. It is possible, through practice and training, to attune your senses and vibrations to a point where you can become physically able to see or sense things which exist on other energy fields or other planes. As mentioned, this is how someone would be able to see the colours of an aura or utilize mediumship capabilities or perform spiritual healings.

As you expand your energy consciousness and your mind, you will automatically go beyond the dense state you are currently functioning in. You may notice that things become subtler, clearer, and easier to perceive with all your senses. As some people begin to glean new information and perceptions, they learn to work with energy. Some experience excitement, even an adrenalin rush, increased energy, and a driving desire to learn more. These exhilarating experiences kick off a continuing flow of energy and build momentum toward their development. I refer to this as the spiral of enlightenment. The more you experience, the more you want to learn and the more dedicated to your development you become.

Thus, energy is a very powerful thing. It is important to remember that the different energy fields are all connected. Following this theory then, something that is done on the physical level is felt on other levels in a ripple effect. Perhaps the most important thing to learn and remember is that *energy follows thought*. Your thoughts have energy. The more you repeat a thought, the more momentum builds towards that thought.

It is important to realize that this works equally for the positive as well as the negative, or even conscious or unconscious thought. As you enter your own spiral of enlightenment, you will realize that you were born with *Divine Power* and that is what separates humankind from the rest of the Earth's creatures. You have a *consciousness,* and the power of your conscious mind is very real. You can manifest things by merely focusing your thoughts and your energy.

Once something has become an actual thought, it has been given life and energy by your conscious and unconscious efforts. Thoughts are things. Therefore, it is very important when seeking to learn more about ourselves, when seeking enlightenment and development, that we become very aware of our thoughts. As your awareness takes hold and begins to expand, so will your consciousness, and your energy potential. But it all begins with your thoughts.

When we open ourselves to the psychic, energetic, or spiritual realms, we find that it is with these subtle non-physical realms of the Universe that all connection and communication with Spirit occurs. This is where intuitive information comes from. It connects to us on a soul level and is filtered through our intuition, into our brains. Messages from Angels, Guides, and loved ones all come via this method.

As we train and hone our senses to become heightened, we can realize and access these subtle realms. This access is expressed or communicated to us through mental and emotional transmissions to the mind and the senses. The spiritual self becomes functioning and actively living through the dense physical form of our bodies. Psychic ability is a simple by-product of spiritual expression through the vehicle of the dense physical body. Spirit and matter are *one* within our human existences.

As I said earlier, once I became spiritually ignited, I had a real thirst for spiritual knowledge. I read anything and everything that I could get my hands on that interested me. I did not have any formal plan at all, and I was not necessarily trying to develop my psychic skills. I just knew there was more, and that there was something to the things I was experiencing. I was aware of Spirit Guides and Angels, but I had no real knowledge of how it all worked. Wanting to learn more, I began to educate myself. As I did that, the Guru in me began to awaken.

## A Story Of Divine Awakening

After my cancer ordeal and the treatment that followed, I looked forward to a summer off. I had managed to save my school year and I was so very happy about that. I returned to playing soccer which felt like a huge accomplishment, and since I had always played quite competitively, it made me feel like I had gotten my life back. During the day, I slept and slept and slept. I gardened and meditated and kept investigating the world of energy. By that Fall, I was excited to return for the final year of school and resume a normal life with my friends. During the third week of my final year, I fell completely asleep in class. I had hit a wall of exhaustion and depletion.

It was decided that I would have to leave school for a semester. I was a bit sad at this, but I consoled myself with the fact that I had at least made it to and through graduation. In my area there was a 5th year of high school called Grade 13. If you wanted to attend university rather than college, you needed this extra high school year. I did want those things as did most of my friends, however Grade 13 was something that could be done at any time and did not interfere with getting your actual high school diploma. I was feeling so poorly I did not argue the decision, so back home I went.

I spent another four months of sleeping, resting, and recovering. I also spent quite a bit of time meditating and learning about all things spiritual. On my own, I studied Celtic spirituality, Hinduism, Buddhism, Paganism, Shamanism, Native Spirituality, and Spiritualism. I convalesced and regained my energy and my health. I allowed the grace of healing to lead me.

I surrendered completely to what my body's needs were and I allowed my mind to be free to explore whatever it wanted to. I created the space for Divine Healing, and I allowed myself to just flow in the stream of it unencumbered by outside expectation or pressure. I look back on this time with great fondness, which given why I was there seems perhaps a bit odd. However, I truly believe that because I embraced my time of healing so fully, it created a robust recovery. It is a lesson I have kept at the forefront of my mind ever since.

It was during this time when I took those months off that I experienced what I remember as being some of my first psychic and mediumship experiences. Looking back, I would say that the decade that began with my illness and led into my late twenties truly was a time of great awakening for me. It was in this period of convalescing that I first experienced the awareness of an *energy being* that was outside of myself. I recall meditating one early morning in my bedroom, and I had the sense that two angels had come in through my window.

It was strange. It felt like it does when someone walks into a room and you know they are there before you look up and see them. I knew these two angels were male and a female and that they were there to protect me. A voice inside my head told me that they were my angels and that they were there for me. I was not required to do anything; they were just there. Assigned to me. That simple. So that was that. I did not try to connect or communicate with them. I just merely accepted that this was what it was.

Over the next little while, I would see if I could tell (feel) if they were in a room with me or not. I just thought that if I could sense a difference then I would know that it was real. It turned out that I could. I never felt the urge to chat to them and I never felt disrupted by them. I knew I only needed to think about them, and I would feel them close by. Quite quickly, I grew to take comfort that these beings were there for me. It seemed all quite harmless to me. I did not think at the time to engage with them any further.

Around this time, there were a few other odd occurrences. I was really investigating Shamanism and Native Spirituality at one point and I decided to do a "stone" meditation. I have always been very connected to nature and as a child, I was always collecting stones and sticks and calling them my friends. To me the general philosophies and premise of those practices seemed very natural and right.

I immediately had an easy affinity to many of the Native spiritual practices. I had always felt that things in nature were living beings. I suppose I knew inherently that all things in nature have an energy that is their own, like a unique fingerprint. One day I decided to place a favorite stone on my solar plexus. This is the third chakra as it turned out, and it was my personal power centre, I found out some years later. I decided that I would try to connect deeper with the spirit that was that stone. I know, who thinks like this, right? Me.

As I lay on my bed with my stone, I concentrated on my breath and fell into a deep meditative state. For all intents and purposes, I went "into" the stone. I began to experience strange sensations. My body temperature became very cool and I began to see things in my mind's eye that were so vivid and real, like I was standing in a glass room with light all around me but the windows were blurry, like old glass. Not once but twice I moved to touch my eyes to make sure they were closed because I was seeing as if they were open.

I did feel on some level, I was accessing the memories of that stone. I felt like I was underwater looking out at the sky above and I knew that this stone had been in a stream or riverbed at some point. It was a lovely calming feeling and I can remember still the weighty-ness of my being, such a grounding feeling and looking through water up to the sky and to the surface of that water. It was very grounding and very magical at the same time. Pure contentment. Very solid yet very alive.

The whole experience seemed to be only moments long but when I came out of the meditation more than two hours had gone by and I knew that I had not fallen asleep. To this day when I really need to ground myself, I remember back to that experience and it is now a very powerful tool that helps me. To this day, to my utter joy, I still collect stones and rocks that speak to me.

Not long after that experience, I was asleep in my bedroom and I awoke in the middle of the night because I felt something enter my room. At first, I thought perhaps it was my two angels, but even before I opened my eyes, I could feel that it was not. I could feel something looming over me and I opened my eyes to look to a space on the ceiling above me. Uncertain of what was going on, I just lay there witnessing as I first did when my two angels came. I could tell that whatever it was this time, it was not *angelic*. There was a definite menacing feeling to it.

## 3. EDUCATE THE GURU IN YOU

For some reason this did not panic me, though I was on high alert. I mustered all the courage I could not to freak out and I lay very still using all my senses to glean what was going on. I could feel this thing, being, whatever it was, trying to check me out, like a dog sniffing the air sensing something that it cannot quite see yet. It was the strangest experience.

After what seemed like forever, though it was likely only seconds, I had had enough. In my mind, I called to my angels requesting their presence (if in fact that was what they were around to do) and sure enough, they came to my side. I felt and knew this rather than seeing anything with my physical eyes. So, the foreign energy left very quickly - I had sensed it was male, and I could feel him take off like there was no tomorrow.

In that moment, I knew without a doubt that there are good and evil forces in the Universe and that light energy will always move the dark energy on. I also knew that I was not wrong about sensing what was what. I did indeed have two angels watching over me for life and these two are with me still decades later and help me every day in my work as a medium.

As mentioned, intuition is an inherent ability that we all have, like an internal language we respond to physiologically and emotionally. It is the language of the soul. It is an immediate awareness by the mind, without reasoning. It is an immediate knowing by the senses or immediate insight without previous knowledge. We are hardwired with it, each of us. It is what links us to the two worlds we live in: spirit and matter. It is something that utilizes all our sensory systems in sometimes profound and mysterious ways. We all have it though often we allow ourselves to override it. How many times have you said to yourself, "If only I had listened to that little voice?" Make no mistake, your intuition is the most significant communication tool that you have.

If you want to develop your intuitive muscles with the aim of developing your spiritual and intuitive gifts, the goal is to train yourself to cultivate your conscious relationship with your intuitive mind to the best of your ability. You want to get yourself to the stage where you are co-existing concurrently in the realm of matter and the realm of subtle energy. Our intuition is the go-between of these realms or dimensions helping us to integrate our being. With time and practice, your spiritual gifts will heighten, and that state of higher awareness will become as natural to you as breathing. Your trust and faith in that awareness will be beyond all doubt and questioning.

Obviously, this does not happen quickly and is certainly not a destination. This is a process, dare I repeat it again, and it requires hard work, dedication, and focused attention. It is a bit like learning to drive. Initially, it can be a little intimidating, but once you get used to the rules and the laws, the feel of the vehicle, and the intensity with which to use the gas pedal and the brakes, you take off. Evolving into your gifts includes some trial and error work. As your experiences are integrated into the memory of mind and soul, transformation begins to happen.

Creating an internal environment to nurture this transformation is where a lot of the initial work happens. Our intuition requires a calm, reflective, peaceful, and ordered internal environment to grow and develop. It takes experience gained through time and applied knowledge to be able to interpret and discern intuitive information correctly. It is something that cannot be forced and so you must learn to surrender to Divine timing. Show up for yourself, do the soul work necessary, and nurture the budding relationship with your intuition. Then surrender and trust that the Universe is supporting your desire for expansion.

The following are two easy techniques that I have used myself for years. They are ways to connect to your soul essence and prepare you for intuitive work. I have also used them both many times out and about in day-to-day life whenever I felt anxious or overwhelmed. They help to reconnect to my soul essence and to tune into my support team of Angels, Guides and Loved Ones. It works wonders when I feel I need some extra help to get through a challenging moment. I hope these techniques will assist you in all of that too, but especially in terms preparing to do your own intuitive work.

## __Intuitive Training Tip #3 - Above and Below Breathing Technique__

This technique will help you to create balanced energy before engaging in any intuitive, meditative, or energy work. Learning to feel grounded and solid, secure within your physical and emotional self when you work intuitively is quite important as it leads to better understanding of your experiences. It helps to reset your energy and vibration and restore vitality. It is a simple practice for connecting with yourself and connecting to the subtle realms.

As the diagram below suggests, as you go through this breathing technique you are consciously, at the appropriate time, connecting your energy, your mind, and your intentions to both the cosmos above you and the earth below you. You are inviting the higher energy of the Universe to connect with you and as you do this, you become open to it. At the same time, you are connecting to the earth beneath you and anchoring yourself (or grounding) to it. This technique will help you to set the stage for being primed to recognize energetic and intuitive impulses from a rooted and grounded place. Above and below. Open to the energies of the Universe above and grounded physically to the earth below. This puts you in the best position energetically for any intuitive work that you may want to practice. I recommend always doing this before any meditation, intuitive, or energy work.

Sit or stand with feet solidly on the ground and with a straight back.

Close your eyes and take several deep breaths to connect consciously with your body and mind.

Bring your awareness into your physical self.

Imagine now that you can breathe directly through the soles of your feet.

Take three or four deep breaths in, up through your feet and visualize breathing out through the top of your head.

Imagine the ripples of each breath circulating their way up through your entire body, cell by cell.

Feel the connection to the earth deep below you as you continue your breathing upwards.

Then move your breath in the opposite direction imagining your breath coming in through the top of your head and flowing through your body, exiting through the bottom of your feet.

With each breath, you are connecting deeply to the Cosmos and to the universal energy source.

When you feel ready, and when your body feels rejuvenated, open your eyes and reconnect with the world in front of you.

Carry this new sense of balance and centeredness with you into your day.

**Cosmic energy**

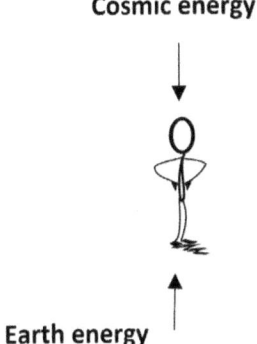

**Earth energy**

## <u>Intuitive Training Tip #4 – Breathing & Visualization Technique</u>

Though I will go into the practice of meditation much deeper later on, this simple technique will introduce you to some basics and incorporates breathing and visualization. Please read through the full steps carefully before trying it yourself. This will make it much easier for you to have a great experience. As you become more familiar with these steps, you can adapt and amend them to your own personal needs. If you are someone who already knows and uses breathing techniques and who meditates daily, view this as a refresher and a way to gain greater context overall.

Take 10 deep breaths in and out directly from your deepest belly.

"Feel" each breath as it goes in and out. Imagine it traveling throughout your body from head to toe.

In your mind, picture a circle of blue or purple light around your body like a loop. Try to feel your entire body, nerve by nerve doing this, and imagine that your breath is feeding each nerve ending with fantastic rejuvenating energy. Imagine this energy moving to any areas of your body that feel tired or tense.

Focus on feeling your hands and feet. Do this for a minimum of 5 breaths in and out.

Feel the energy from your feet connect into the center of the planet and imagine growing roots from your feet and legs into the earth. Do this for a minimum of 5 deep breaths, in and out. You are growing these roots from every area of your body directly into the earth.

Feel the connection to the earth and ask the Universe to take you where you need to go, and just allow yourself to experience what you are sensing in any way. Enjoy the journey and try not to have any expectations. Just relax and breathe.

When you feel ready, just bring your awareness back into your body. Sense the room and where you are physically. Continue breathing slowly and deeply. When you are ready, open your eyes.

Once you feel ready, stretch yourself out. I recommend making a journal entry or note to remember your experience. Don't forget to mark down the date. It is important to keep a record of your experience so that you can track your progress over time.

## **Quick Recap:**

Developing intuitively means understanding that both you and the world around you are comprised of different energetic levels. Some of these are obvious, and some of them are subtle. Your whole being, the physical, mental, emotional, and spiritual aspects of you, are all part of the communication process. You have a deep connection with the subtle realms of the Universe, things which your eye cannot see. These subtle realms influence how you act and react, because the physical realm, our dense physical world, is the last point of integration. Things happen on the subtle realms first, and then finally on this plane. Thus, it serves you to become as aware of the subtle realms as you can be, and this is where developing your intuition will help.

You are made up of several different energy fields that maintain a constant individual activity and vibration. As you grow and learn in life your consciousness is moved along a spiral of enlightenment. As your knowledge and self-knowledge expand, so does your awareness. You are a very powerful being and you control your own experience by how you choose to perceive things. Your energy follows your thoughts, and as such, your thoughts have energetic power and momentum that grow as your consciousness expands.

When it comes to connecting and communicating with the Spirit realm, to your Angels and Guides, know that it all comes from the subtle realm through your intuition and into your brain. When you sense something intuitively, there is an immediate comprehension by your mind without any logic or reasoning. Intuitive knowing is an immediate thing. You just know. There is no thinking involved. So, as you are practicing, use that as a gauge to measure your intuitive vibes and information.

# 4. KNOW THE GURU IN YOU

## 4. KNOW THE GURU IN YOU

You may be sensing that the initial work involved in developing your intuition is primarily internal. You are correct. Therefore, it is not possible to evolve your intuitive skills without evolving yourself. There is a direct correlation between the successful progression of your intuitive skills and that of your physical, mental, emotional, and spiritual health and wellbeing. Think of your physical body as the wi-fi connection, your intuition as the modem and your brain as your laptop. You will see that the better quality of the wi-fi, the clearer the signal to the modem is, and therefore the higher the quality, speed and accuracy the information to the laptop is.

As you actively work to awaken the Guru in you, you'll become aware of this process: knowing yourself, creating a strong foundation, and building a relationship with spirit. It is important to understand that cultivating your intuitive ability cannot be forced by will or desire alone. The awakening, opening, and development of this latent ability has as much to do with personal growth and self-development as with anything else, and often people pay the least attention to this and wonder why things do not progress. If you find yourself blocked in your gifts in any way, I suggest you set your desire for these gifts aside for a time and focus on your own personal and spiritual growth. Desire is just ego getting ahead of itself and when that happens, your desire can become a roadblock.

You do not have to manifest your spiritual potential in a specific way. For example, some people want to be able to see spirits and talk to people who have passed on, or they want to have clairvoyance and be able to know future things. When you have truly mastered knowing yourself and continue to grow and align with your spiritual self, these abilities will unfold naturally. There is no point setting your sights on how or when it should happen. The minute you try to control anything or attach to a certain way that a thing should *unfold*, you have tipped the balance in the ego department and are setting up blocks for yourself.

Intuitive and psychic ability very often come as a by-product of a spiritual path or spiritual practice. To truly find and know yourself, you will come to know the Divine and the spiritual realms. Only then will you be able to develop psychically in balance and with success. Power or ability without self-mastery, self-control, purity of spirit, and intention is ultimately a recipe for self-destruction. Cultivating self-knowledge is the best way to enhance your life and benefit others.

The concept of knowing yourself is also called *self-actualization* and there is a wealth of information available out there that can offer you endless ways to achieve this. When you do begin to work with your spirituality, all the effort you invest in yourself helps you in that personal development work. If you want to learn to communicate with the Spirit world through Guides, Angels, Loved Ones, understand that all your accumulated knowledge will be utilized. Nothing you do in life is ever a waste of time or energy.

## 4. KNOW THE GURU IN YOU

Are you wondering why this matters so much? It's because connecting and working with Spirit is all about awareness. The deeper your knowledge of internal things is, the sharper and more defined your awareness of external things will become. This will increase your ability to sense and discern information from the dense and subtle realms. Your intuition is a compass meant to help you navigate life to the highest potential. The better you know yourself, the better the compass works.

I find one of the best ways to move forward on this is to take stock of where I am at on all levels. I am always assessing my physical, mental, emotional, and spiritual self. It may sound annoying or boring, but it really helps me to keep my mind and my intentions clear. Just like cleaning the windows, I like to keep my mind as grime-free as possible.

I do this by asking myself a bunch of questions. Sometimes I will sit in meditation contemplating one or two. Sometimes I will journal some of them. Often when I am out for a walk, I will have a conversation with myself and chat about it all. This may be a whole new concept for you however I believe that most people already spend time doing this. I like to have a take-charge attitude with self-reflection though because I know how important it is to be clear on where I am at in life and how much this helps me in my intuitive work.

Some of the questions I ask myself are things such as how honest am I being with myself, or questions about a specific situation. What are some of the core beliefs that are driving my intentions or decisions? How am I doing at expressing self-love and taking care of my health and nutrition? How am I sleeping lately? Am I feeling in balance with things in my life?

If you were to assess your physical, mental, emotional, and spiritual well-being today, what would that look like? Do you have a spiritual reflective or meditation practice and do you practice daily? As I have said, these things will impact your ability to get the most potential from your spiritual gifts. Deepen your relationship with yourself and you will deepen your relationship with the world of Spirit. This will lead to the development of your intuition and your spiritual gifts more than anything else.

Once you have awareness, there is no turning back. This is perhaps why some people choose not to look at themselves too closely, because they fear change. Change is imminent and we must accept this. To grow, things must change, and we must change with them. We always have a choice, but to resist growth is to stagnate. If you feel stuck somewhere in your life, I suspect with some honest investigation you will find that you are resisting growth on some level. I suggest you embrace the energy of a spiritual warrior, choose to become fearless in your pursuit of self-knowledge and self-awareness. This is a key factor in enhancing your relationship with Spirit and developing your intuitive skills.

Conscious living is the result of knowing yourself deeply. The awareness that comes from dedicated reflection ultimately makes its presence known in your thoughts, and in your self-observation. You come to realize that the power of your thoughts and your imagination are what create your experiences and thus your reality. Remember that energy follows thought and focused thoughts create our experience. As you begin to deepen your self-knowledge, you will notice that your awareness expands. You will notice that you are able to sense the nuances of energy that you come in and move out of. For example, you may be able to get a quicker sense of what is going on in your work, or a better sense of when it is the right or wrong time to act on something in a given situation. You may begin to have an awareness of your own patterns and actions, and with that will be able to make life changes quicker than you have done in the past. These are all signs that you are increasing your mind power and your inner knowing. All are signs that you are living more intuitively.

As you begin to live more intuitively and prove yourself to yourself, you will find that you develop as new sense of trust and confidence in yourself, especially in decision making and also in trusting that you are reading or gauging a situation correctly. You will rely on confirmation from outside sources less and less as you begin to trust yourself more and more. Eventually you will get to a place where all you will need to trust something is your own intuitive nudge that what you are experiencing is exactly what you think it is. Less questioning, more accepting that you know what is true and untrue for yourself. This is exactly what happened to me and is exactly why when I have experienced some things that may seem *out there* to others, I do not question these myself. I know what I know, intuitively speaking.

## **A Story Of Divine Trust**

The following year or so after my cancer time, I had two very intense experiences which I have trouble defining. In both cases, I was consciously taken to another time, back in time as it happens. I know this will challenge some people's beliefs, but I can only tell you my experience. In both cases I was awake and in an active state. I was physically doing something at the time these things happened. Thus, the one thing I do know is that they were not dreams, because I was awake and active both times.

In each case, I was witnessing myself and watching myself interact with that self's surroundings. As I did this, I experienced immediate insight. More importantly as I watched myself in what I believed to be past life scenarios, I knew I was witnessing something very important and relevant to my current life. Specifically, I was given insights to my current relationships with the same people who were in each of the past life scenarios. It became clear that I had some karma to deal with and I was being warned as to what patterns were being repeated and were playing out in my present-day life.

I know, this all sounds a little science-fiction like and may seem a stretch of the imagination. It's true when they say that life is stranger than fiction. For me in this situation that was certainly the case. There are a lot of theories about past lives. There are even theories about multiple lives co-existing at the same time and even quantum leaping between these lives. This however is not the place for discussing such things. I certainly do not have all the answers about it all. I can only say that personally I do believe in past lives and I have had many experiences in my life that support my belief. I can tell you that it was my perception at the time that I was indeed witnessing what seemed to me to be past life experiences in a 3D kind of format, and that these experiences helped me greatly. I believe that the Universe is infinitely intelligent and regardless of what it was technically that I experienced, it helped me tremendously.

Essentially, I was shown two past lives in a very tactile physical way and both experiences helped me to deal with situations that were about to unfold in my current life. The first revelation was that a relationship I was in at the time was actually a replay of karma from a previous lifetime and I was being shown that the same pattern was repeating itself. In the past, I had been used by this person for my skills and my power and that was

## 4. KNOW THE GURU IN YOU

what was at the root of the relationship issues I was currently struggling with.

In the second case, a similar thing was happening. I was being held captive because my captor needed something energetically from me that they could not find in anyone else. Sure enough I could see a clear link between this captive situation from the past with that soul and what was happening in my current reality in my intimate relationship in this lifetime.

I think of these experiences as a gift. They were quite disturbing at the moment I was shown them, but they were undeniably useful to me in helping me navigate a couple of very difficult situations. To be honest, I have never needed to look beyond that. In the moment, I recognized the information as a gift and was grateful for the heads-up from the Universe. I embraced it all with Divine Trust and took the message not needing to know more.

Within a few months after this, I enrolled in a course of study that was to me a new form of meditation. It involved spending three hours a day in practice and study at a Thai Buddhist Temple near where I lived and worked. I was very much ignited by this course of study and I moved mountains to make sure that I could participate. Every weekday for six months that is what I did. At the end of that term of study, there was to be a class trip to Thailand. At the time, our teacher was an 84-year-old Thai Buddhist monk who spread his time between Canada and Thailand. The course was free. Talk about an inspiration!

I cannot tell you what this experience did for me. It was so powerful in so many ways. I can tell you that I got further in six months using this meditation technique than I had in the previous 15 years of meditating by myself. At this time, I was single again and about 32 years of age. I was still working in my corporate marketing job and still doing tarot readings. I had begun to teach a spiritually-based meditation course on my own and was still working at times with a psychic acquaintance as well as some other spiritual and healer type people.

I was really working hard at developing my intuition rather than specific psychic ability. I had already begun to recognize that intuition was the key to it all and my only interest in the psychic stuff was to help people. I have never been much concerned with the hocus pocus parlour trick psychic world to be honest. It was never my thing to get caught up in that stuff.

Unfortunately, my position on this began to be a problem for other people. The ego is a funny thing and some people get very caught up in it. The timing of my attending the meditation course was important as it coincided with my arrival at a decision to stop doing psychic parties with small groups in people's homes. It was not really something I felt good about for many reasons.

To start with, my job was very demanding, and I had to work extra hours so that I could attend my meditation course. The last thing I wanted to do on a Saturday was sit and do tarot readings for hours and hours at someone's house. Those parties paid pretty well, but it was never about the money for me. Then I learned in the meditation course how this type of psychic activity was very detrimental to the development of one's mind power. Well, that was it. That knowledge was all I needed to stop doing reading parties and group readings for good.

The decision to stop was not met with support by my fellow partner that I did the parties with. In fact, it started a whole massive drama that involved several of my spiritual peers and was very messy indeed. All through that drama, I knew it was all happening for important reasons and again, I embraced Divine Trust believing it was all leading me to something that was better for me.

In the end, certain relationships ceased, and certain individuals exposed their true natures as always happens as time rolls on. Fortunately, this did not damage me as some would have liked. It certainly taught me a lot. To this day, I have never done another reading party and I limit my client work, which allows me to balance my mind power keeping me very energetically strong. I also no longer question my instincts about people or about things I do not want to be involved with.

As you begin to develop your intuitive skills, it is crucial to develop a strong foundation at the same time. By this I mean building your mind power which is your mental and energetic strength. Your intuitive gifts are only as strong as your mind's ability to receive the information and discern that information with clarity and without ego. Always trust your instincts and your intuition. It is your built-in guidance system and it will never lead you astray.

Sometimes as you begin to open psychically, your ego can get the best of you. I have known more than one person who was convinced they were Ascended Masters here on earth because they received a message in a meditation and misinterpreted the information. Maybe they were, however, I believe it more likely they were not fully grounded in their mental discernment and unbalanced in their ego. What I do know is that working on yourself and becoming skilled at sustaining a laser focus in your intuitive work will improve your life exponentially.

I know I keep saying it, but the importance of balanced living cannot be overstated. A life of balance and moderation is both necessary and vital to intuitive development because it helps to cultivate and sustain the creative energy and life force that keeps you in a higher vibration. This higher vibration is needed to ensure and maintain your connection to the spiritual realm as well as ensuring its purity, integrity, and clarity. Through that vibration, a strong and powerful current exists. It is from this current that spiritual and intuitive gifts flow.

I believe my years of meditation laid the proper foundation for my intuitive gifts to flourish. Through my illness too, I spent a lot of time and energy in contemplation which lent itself to know myself very deeply. I had a strong sense of self and because of that, I was able to really embrace Divine trust in my experiences. I was also able to stay quite grounded when challenging things unexpectedly unfolded for me. Investing in yourself is always going to be an investment that pays you back tenfold. I encourage you to give yourself the gift of alone time and of contemplation. Try to spend time reflecting on your life with an eye to gleaning positive insights from past experiences. Approach your life with a deep internal honesty and before you know it, you will be trusting yourself like you have never done before.

## Intuitive Training Tip #5 - Foundational Inquiry Technique:

Self-reflection is always difficult and time consuming, especially if it is something that you are not used to doing. I have found it to be such a worthwhile practice however, and I urge you to give it a try. The best way to know yourself is to educate yourself by bringing focused attention to analyzing your thoughts and habits and taking time to examine your beliefs. For example, if you have always had issues around money, have you ever

## 4. KNOW THE GURU IN YOU

wondered where that came from? Is there a reason for that issue that you can think of, or is it perhaps an issue you have inherited from your family? The best way to know the Guru in you is to spend some time with yourself examining your life. I often do this by taking walks in nature or even doing housework. There are always lots of opportunities to engage on focused thought, you just have to decide to do it. This is part of how you *do the work* that leads to increasing your intuition.

You can use the following questions as journal prompts or a thought exercise to gauge where you are at as you begin to deepen your self-knowledge. Your responses will help you to gauge where you are at now and to keep you on track. This technique also helps you to learn how to properly act on your energetic and intuitive impulses.

- Do you know when your ego is getting in the way?

- How deeply have you examined your intentions in terms of why you want to develop and how you are developing?

- How much time do you spend reflecting or meditating?

- How easily does other people's energy impact or affect you?

- How long is your ability to hold a concentrated focus and how quickly or easily do you get distracted?

- How easy is it for you to sit still?

- How easy is it for you to be in silence?

- How difficult is it for you to be in a noisy environment?

- How often do you feel like you are on an emotional rollercoaster?

- How is your memory these days?

- How are you sleeping? How difficult is it for you to relax?

- How are your stress management strategies working? Do you have any?

These things all will affect your intuitive ability. These things will improve as you start to notice them daily and use your mind power to work on them. You need to be able to control your mind at will and to know the path that thought takes, as well as the impact that thought has on your physical body. The goal is to use your mind's power to successfully increase the strength of your spiritual and intuitive gifts.

## **Quick Recap:**

It seems obvious, the deeper you know yourself the more success you will have in life and the more intuitive you will become. That deep knowledge is truly a gateway to creating a strong foundation and building a relationship with spirit. These are the keys to awakening your intuitive and spiritual gifts.

Though this may seem obvious I can assure that it is the one area where I have seen people fail time and time again. They wonder why they are not improving in intuitive growth, yet they are not spending enough time getting real with themselves about themselves. They are not spending any time in contemplation and they are not taking good care of their physical vehicle. Cultivating your intuitive ability cannot be forced by will or desire alone. You have to do the work if you want to improve,

## 4. KNOW THE GURU IN YOU

plain and simple. If you find yourself blocked in any way, set your desires aside for a time and focus on your own personal and spiritual growth.

Much of intuitive and psychic ability comes as a by-product of a spiritual path or spiritual practice. Reflection, contemplation, and meditation are significant factors in determining the success of your intuitive practice. It can sound daunting, but it's as simple as spending regular time in conversation with yourself. Ability without self-mastery, self-control, purity of spirit, and intention is a recipe for personal disaster. Your intuitive gifts will only ever be as strong as your mind's ability to receive and discern information with clarity and without ego. If you live a heathy balanced life of moderation and spend some time educating yourself about yourself and how you interact with the world around you, you will ace intuitive living. You will be happier than you ever dreamed you could be.

# 5. ESTABLISH THE GURU IN YOU

## 5. ESTABLISH THE GURU IN YOU

How do you define Spirit? If you define Spirit as something that is outside yourself, apart from you or above you, you will always feel that it is something higher, something to be reaching for or grasped at. However, if you recall that our human vessel embodies both Spirit and matter then you will know you are already there. You are already connected to and a part of Spirit. Keep this at the forefront of your thoughts in your pursuit of knowing and building your relationship with all things of Spirit. Recall that your beliefs have a direct impact on your perception and how you experience all your relationships and your life.

When communicating or working with Spirit intuitively, remember that in receiving your messages and insights, the energy may *feel* like it is coming from a source outside of yourself and at the same time, it is connected to you on some deep level. You may not have prior knowledge of something and yet know it to be true. It is not outside you at all because everything is connected to each other and to the Universe. Intuition is the name for that *knowing*.

You may experience a knowing by just simply sensing something. Alternatively, you may experience a speaking voice in your mind or head, and you may even see a flash or an image or colour. Whatever method it is that you begin to sense your intuitive information, know that it is all your intuition at work. We are all wired differently and have a unique way of communicating with the world around us. Just let it all unfold and judge each experience on its own merit. Eventually you will figure out exactly how your intuitive skills work, so until then just be open and pay attention. All of this is how you will begin to establish the guru in you.

Learning to work with, trust, respect, use, and navigate your intuition is what awakens the Guru in you and brings out your spiritual gifts. This is done by building your mindpower, strengthening your foundation, and honing your focus. As you work in conscious partnership with your intuition, let your *soul* be your coach along the way. It will guide you and connect with you. Your soul is the seat of your higher consciousness and of your intuition.

Start with small things. Don't limit your experience with expectation and ego. Ask your soul, mind, and spirit to lead you to things, to reveal answers, to bring solutions to you, to find a parking space even! Learning to trust your soul and allowing your soul to become your coach is how you begin to build a relationship with Spirit. Doing this will build your trust in the intuitive process, and as the connection deepens, it will strengthen and grow, and your gifts will reveal themselves.

Practice and work with Spirit via your intuition as part of your regular daily activities. Acknowledge your connection with Spirit every day. Tune in and tune up! Remember that everything is connected. There can never be any disconnection.

It is not possible. Even if you *feel* disconnected sometimes. If you do feel disconnected, check within yourself to see what is out of balance. The answer will be within you.

Remember this is a process and it takes time. There is always a trial and error period when you are learning new things and beginning to work intuitively is no different. As you work to establish the guru in you, know that if you are doing your part by practicing and learning to become aware, the Universe will meet you halfway. You will get signs and encouragement along the way. You will never get more than you can handle and therefore you should not worry about any of it. Divine Timing is always in the lead. We can want something deeply, but if it is not the right time for us to have it, it will not be there for us. As well, as you develop remember that you are always in control.

I have this expression called *the death fear*. I use it to describe a feeling that is beyond scared. The kind of fear that paralyses you; the kind where you stop breathing and freeze like a dear in the headlights. I share this next experience to ease and allay any fears you may have about beginning to awaken your intuitiveness. I have only experienced this feeling a couple of times in my life and only once did it have anything to do with my psychic or development. I share it now to illustrate my point above, that you are always in control. You are always the boss of you!

## A Story Of Divine Timing

During the same post cancer period I have been sharing, a final experience still stands out for me. I used to think about it negatively, as a place where I got myself off track. I love sleeping but once again, in the middle of the night, I was awoken from a happy slumber. This time I was being shaken awake. I felt a firm hand on my shoulder shaking me and waking me up. I was sure it was my Dad. "What?" I complained. "What is it?" To my surprise, it was not my father. In fact, no one at all was there. As I looked up to the logical place. Where a person would be standing, instead I saw a glowing shimmering floating ball of light. Well, that was it for me! I freaked out. I swear I thought I would literally die of fright. I had the *death fear*. I stared at the floating ball (which of course I now know was an orb) and I wanted to be OK with it, but my response was more of a *hell no* than anything else. Like I had done once before when I was 10 years old and my dead grandfather's giant technicolor floating head had woke me up, I turned my back on the orb and said "No." I prayed immediately to Jesus to come and to make it stop; make the orb and all of it just stop. And so, it all did.

It seems I was OK with meditation and even OK with knowing energy beings were around me, but I was so not OK with seeing apparitions of any kind. This was long before I knew anything about mediumship or psychic gifts. Up to this point, it had all been about connecting to nature and energy, and meditation. I was totally alright with those things and I was very strong in my faith as well. This type of thing, the floating orbs, were not within my comfort zone. Even today I would have to say this kind of stuff is still way out of my comfort zone, which is more than likely why I do not see spirit in a physical sense too often. I just don't think my heart could take it. It's so not a logical thing.

In the meantime, I just got on with life and trusted that if I was meant to do anything more with that stuff, God would take care of it and let me know. I gave it all up to Divine timing. I kept meditating, reading, learning, and following my spiritual path and did not think much about anything psychic. When I was ready, the Universe bought it all back to me and that is how Divine Timing works. It is true what they say: what is meant for you will not pass you by.

## 5. ESTABLISH THE GURU IN YOU

As time went on and it all came back around, I found myself in an Etheric Healing Level 2 class. I had begun to work with tarot card readings as I mentioned previously. I was comfortable with this and had for years continued to work with my Guides and Angels in a spiritual way. A friend at the time invited me the Level 2 class. I was a bit unsure as it was a second level course in something that I had never heard of before, and I certainly did not have Level 1, but that did not seem to bother anyone.

The class began and I knew immediately that I was totally out of my depth. I had no clue what they were discussing. "What's a chakra?" I asked with uncertainty. I was told it was an energy centre in your body and luckily, I could relate it to *power centers* that I had read about in my Native and Eastern spirituality books. Then I was told we were going to do a guided meditation. Once again, I asked "What is that?" I was told not to worry about it, just to close my eyes and listen to the instructor's voice guiding me. Alrighty, I thought.

This was not too far out there for me since I was quite used to meditating. I just followed along and got into a meditative state as part of the group. Then basically I just paid attention to what my own experience was regardless of what the facilitator was saying. In this meditation, at some point, I was having a meditative conversation with Jesus. He had appeared to me before in meditation, so that was not all that unusual for me. It was always a meaningful and wonderful experience. All seemed to be fine and going well until we came out of the meditation.

I opened my eyes a little before others and happened to see the moment the instructor came out of it. Well, her head snapped in my direction so fast I was sure she would have hurt her neck. I saw her face and her expression, and I thought, goodness, I am in big trouble. She knows that I have not studied Level 1 and should not really be here. I thought for sure I was in for it. After she recovered from herself, she merely went on with the class until it was time for lunch.

We went as a class to lunch, and nothing was really said to me. My friend and I ended up being separated and she sat with the instructor. On the way back, she told me the teacher had said to her, "So your friend is pretty connected?" Now I honestly had not known this friend for very long, so I do not know what she thought about it all. I however gleaned that somehow, she must have known who was in my meditation with me and that is when I began to understand about empathic energy and how important psychic awareness is in that kind of atmosphere.

I was hopeful that this woman was going to become a mentor and teacher for me who would help me achieve new heights spiritually. I was still feeling uneasy about being in a Level 2 class having not done the first level so after the class was finished, I approached the instructor about it. She laughed at me, in a loving manner, and said, "Oh, I think you don't have to worry about that. You seem to be very connected." The way she was looking at me I knew she knew about the Jesus thing. My secret was out, sort of.

I asked her point blank if she was meant to be my teacher and mentor and she said, "Oh no dear, I am not your teacher." I was so disappointed because I was really hoping to find a teacher to help me advance. My feelings must have shown on my face because she continued: "You need to understand. Your teachers are not here on earth. They are in the higher planes." And that was that. I figured I would investigate the whole chakra thing because that seemed to be important in terms of learning healing skills and I would continue studying on my own as I always had done.

## 5. ESTABLISH THE GURU IN YOU

Soon afterward I was doing a reading party for some women, back when I was still involved in those parties. One of the women was a very left-brained person, an accountant, and she was a bit of a skeptic. I was OK with that; I had come across that before. It was a very interesting moment for me, one where my understanding of Divine Timing was deepened and my faith in Divine Trust reaffirmed. In the reading for her, I could tell that this woman was very much in need of healing around the passing of her mother and of that relationship in general. I could feel the presence of her mother with us in the room. This was really the first time that I consciously was aware of and open to a person in Spirit connecting directly with me in a reading.

As you may recall in an earlier story, I was not comfortable with the whole medium thing and I knew I did not want to see any apparitions since that never goes down well with me. But I knew that this woman would never accept the things that I was telling her and certainly never accept that they were from her mother unless she had the tactile proof she needed.

In my communication with the spirit of her mother, I gave permission for her to use my body to prove her presence to her daughter. I allowed it. I felt her come into my physical body and I did as she directed me to do. It was as if a zipper was put into my body. She unzipped and stepped halfway into my body. The right side of my body went ice cold. The left side of my body was warm.

I commentated to my client as this was happening and invited her to feel the two halves of my body with her hands to compare. It did not take long before the tears started to roll. A great healing happened that day and I was grateful for that. I also learned a few things that day. What I allowed to happen is something called Trans-mediumship, and I learned it is nothing that I am interested in doing again. I did however realize that the timing was now right for me to embrace my gifts in a new way. I went home and finished that book that had freaked me out 6 months earlier and I stopped doing tarot readings and began to embrace my path as a medium. I had a deepened understanding of and trust in Divine Timing.

As you practice listening to your intuitive voice and acting on its urges, you will begin to see that cultivating a relationship with your intuition and higher-self works much like any other relationship. There are always some key things to keep in mind to ensure that you stay happy and productive as your relationship grows and blossoms.

A good relationship is based on *trust*. Without complete trust, a pure intuitive relationship cannot be cultivated. This takes time. Begin slowly and allow yourself time to learn what works and does not work for you. Keep things simple. Try taking a different route to work. Try choosing a new dressing or sauce from purely intuitive instinct – no label reading! Prove yourself to yourself over and over and over. Then over again. Absolute faith in the process is crucial and you need to surrender to it and allow it to evolve.

*Integrity and intention* are also key things to keep in mind. Be true to yourself. If you can't be integral with yourself, trust will never happen. If you aren't the kind of person who would lie to your loved ones, then don't lie to yourself. What are your intentions, and do they match that of Divine will? Are you acting from your heart and from a sense of service, or is ego in

## 5. ESTABLISH THE GURU IN YOU

charge? Honesty equals results. What is your role of personal responsibility in this work?

As I have previously stated, a message is only received to the degree that its receptor is healthy and *balanced*. Your physical body is a walking receptor. Therefore, you need hydration, rest, whole natural food, fresh air, and some exercise. You need to manage stress. When you do these things for yourself with regularity, you will be ready to correctly interpret your body's signals. Create balance in your life. You will be happier and more intuitive. Small changes lead to big transformations.

There is so much to learn from *stillness* and *quiet*. Clarity cannot come in the midst of internal or external chaos. Find fifteen minutes, a couple of times a day, to sit still and just be. Have a seat in the shower even. It is very relaxing, and the kids can't get in if you lock the door! Sit. Be quiet. Be still. This is the first step in learning to be *in* your body with conscious awareness. This is the first step in intuitive communication. Work at that relationship. Learn to be still in your mind. Learn to move into intuition from a place of emotional neutrality, sensing emotion without having to feel it too deeply. It will take time to get good at this, so always give yourself understanding and compassion as you are learning.

Awareness takes time and patience and it has multiple levels. Become a master at detecting nuances. Work at feeling the subtleties and nuance of energy. This begins within your mind and your physical body first, and then outside. Make it game – a fun thing. Next time you are in a full room or a board meeting – or even a family dinner – just sit back, keep quiet and notice it all. I guarantee you that there is a whole undiscovered world sitting under your nose in the energy of the room. Work at this and you will master the most important skill required to cultivate the unfailing inner wisdom of your intuition: *awareness*.

With all these new learnings, you will naturally be integrating your new knowledge. It's all a process. Do not forget this. Just because you've decided to invite intuitiveness in your life doesn't mean that the response will be immediate. This is not something that can be forced or created by will or desire. Try that and you will never develop. Remember it is a Divine and sacred relationship you are building with yourself. Relax and enjoy the process of *integration* without expectation. Divine timing is what rules. You are just the instrument. Intuition must be developed. It works with reason and intellect as a partner.

You may feel that you are being sabotaged sometimes but it's probably from ego. The ego is something we all wrestle with and is challenging to grasp sometimes. I often think part of ego is that side of ourselves that makes us fear and doubt and clouds our perception sometimes. *Ego* often gets a bad rap however, without a certain amount of healthy ego, we would not even get out of bed in the morning. We need ego to thrive and to live life to its fullest. We do not however need an ego that is out of balance. That is never a good thing. Awareness of self is always a bit of a double-edged sword. Naturally as we begin to pay close attention and scrutinize ourselves, we run the risk of noticing things that aren't so hot.

This is opportunity knocking. Don't play mental gymnastics with yourself – put your ego on a leash. Truly, you need to get to a place where you are ready to receive information whether your ego mind is ready to hear it or not. Sometimes you may be surprised by the information you receive. The trick is not to let ego and emotional expectation manipulate the information into something that you want it to be or that you fear it might be. This is a tough one. *Tough*. My advice is to call yourself on your shit. Build in a time to ensure you think about things and weigh them up. Is there a place ego might be getting the better of you, and if so, what are you going to do about it? Are you seeing what you want to see or are you seeing things as they really are? How is your discernment and how are you keeping it in check? Make sure to have a check and balance contemplation often, as part of your regular meditation practice.

So now many messages are perhaps coming at you, but are you acting on your intuitive nudges and confirming for yourself that your intuitiveness is growing and working? *Action* is part of building the trust in the relationship with your intuition. Follow-through is just as crucial as getting the information and insight. When you follow through, not only are you proving yourself to yourself, but you are telling all the Guides, Angels and Helpers in Spirit that you want to keep participating and that you are doing your part. Remember it is like all relationships: give and take. You have to let the Universe know that you are showing up ready and willing to do the work and acting on the information you intuit!

I have mentioned before how critical proper *discernment* is when working intuitively. Proper discernment it built on certain skills that are all part and parcel of working successfully with your intuition. We have mentioned trust, and that applies here too. You have to be able to get yourself to a place where you believe in your ability and you easily trust the messages you receive. This will come with practice. It is equally important to make sure that when you are engaging in intuitive work that your own energy is balanced. It does not pay to try to work intuitively if you are distracted with big emotion. Aim to work only from a place of emotional neutrality and you will get the best information. Remember the more balanced you are on the whole (physically, mentally, emotionally, and spiritually), the more *clarity* you will have.

Be open, be neutral, and trust that you will receive intuitive information. What you want to ensure more than anything is the information you receive *is relevant and useful.* Otherwise, what is the point? When you sharpen all these skills *before* you begin looking for intuitive clues or information, know that you will receive the right kind of information. When you act on it, you will show yourself and the Universe your desire to work as partners, and then look out, you will become an intuitive badass!

## **Intuitive Training Tip #6 - Practice Tuning into Yourself**

Choose a time, any time of the day or night, to try this technique. In fact, try this as many different times as you can. Sit for a moment and take a couple of deep breaths. Ask yourself one very simple question and go with the first thing that comes into your mind. If you feel encouraged to explore deeper, journal your answers and see if you can expand on your first impressions. Practice listening to your intuitive voice. These little exercises will really help you learn to connect to your intuitive voice.

A few suggestions are:

- What is my deepest desire right now?

- What does my inner self really want for me now?

- What do I need to know most about _____ situation right now?

Expand the questions into any area of your life you wish. Just keep making sure that you are neutral, open, well intended, and still and calm in your mind. Practice makes perfect! Start small and branch out as you go. This will help you to understand your individual process and build your confidence. Keep taking action and you will see results.

## **Quick Recap:**

As you begin to work intuitively and begin connecting to Spirit in various ways, it is very important to know you are always connected to Spirit; it is a part of you. There is never any disconnection. You are a spiritual being on a human journey.

Building your mind power, strengthening your physical, mental, emotional, and spiritual foundations, including honing your focus will all help to awaken your intuition. Trust, integrity, intention, balance, stillness, quiet, and awareness are all considerations when doing this work and are all part of the intuitive unfolding process. Integration of all of these takes time and you will experience periods of trial and error. It is the same for everyone and is totally normal.

As you go through this process be mindful of keeping your ego in check. Learn to *put yourself on a shelf.* Keep your mind as neutral as possible when doing your intuitive work. If you do this, your discernment will become sharp and clear. When you take action such as meditating, journaling, and connecting to your higher self and your soul, you are telling your intuitive self that you trust it and want to work with it. Taking action and responsibility for yourself invites intuition into your life.

# 6. CULTIVATE THE GURU IN YOU

## 6. CULTIVATE THE GURU IN YOU

I am often asked how I developed intuitively, psychically, and also more generally people wonder, how I maintain my sense of calm and happiness. For me, the answer is meditation for all of it. If pressed I would say that meditation has been the single most influential tool that I have learned in life, and that the biggest gift of meditation for me was the sharpening of my discernment. I feel like my discernment is my super-power along with faith, and my practice of walking and sitting meditation is what gave me this super-power and what helps me to keep it sharp. It is what gives me my confidence in life, underpins my ability to successfully work as a psychic and medium, and maintains my health and happiness. You never know what life if going to throw at you, but if you embrace self-responsibility and work hard, you will be able to handle it all. I feel my discernment is what is at the core of my intuitiveness and I feel like it has saved my life many times over.

How exactly is intuition cultivated, you may wonder. In my experience, it is part practice and part discipline. It is also about paying attention as you experience life. There are lessons and opportunities being presented to us constantly in our everyday lives. Recognizing and learning from your experiences and lessons also helps with intuitive development.

It all starts with a daily meditation has the power to transform your life in a multitude of ways. It is part of the alchemy of life, giving us all the ability to transform, not metal to gold, but misery, conflict, and neurosis into happiness and joy. Its process is so subtle, and yet its force is so powerful that given the proper time and effort, it will penetrate every aspect of your life. A *meditation practice* will connect you to your higher self, your *source*. With this sustained connection you will quickly see positive changes in your life as well as increased intuition.

Initially these changes may be small and subtle, but they will become more and more obvious with time. You will feel a new sense of internal and external awareness and eventually develop a deep knowing and clarity about your life, certainty about your life. You will begin to recognize that you are the power that directs your life. You will learn that you are not merely what your emotions or thoughts are, and that you have real power.

One of the most important factors in developing your intuition, as you learn to trust and successfully use it, is ensuring that you have a strong mental foundation. A strong mind can focus, discern, and articulate effectively, efficiently, and clearly with ease. A strong mind does not get caught up in emotion which can impede and influence intuitive impression and insight. These are the essential skills of intuitive development. They become even more imperative as your intuitive sensitivities expand into higher psychic realms. They are what you want to keep razor sharp if you have the desire to deepen your intuitive skills and develop clairvoyance or mediumship.

In its simplest explanation, meditation is a form of self-discipline that when practiced and mastered will lead to an expansion of consciousness. Meditation is about bringing your physical, mental, and emotional states into harmony and balance, then

## 6. CULTIVATE THE GURU IN YOU

learning to *access* and *direct* the energy, or life force, that comes with that harmony. Within that balance is the *source* of true personal power. Through the practice of meditation, you will learn to connect with the source, *your source*. The more adept and practiced you become at meditation, the further you will expand your conscious awareness and you will experience more and more amazing things.

Make no mistake, meditation is an inward journey. It is not a means of escaping who you are but rather a means of discovering *who* and *what* you are at the deepest possible levels. The way to personal freedom points inwards, not outwards. This includes all the good, the bad, and the ugly, as well as the beautiful and the divine. It all must be recognized, acknowledged, and witnessed before it can be transcended and transformed.

If we try to deny or repress any part of ourselves, we do ourselves a grave injustice and will likely become even more distracted by the very things we are trying to avoid. Meditation is not about fixing anything, but rather about acknowledging what already exists within us and ultimately deciding what to do or what not to do with that information. The mind power built in meditation is what helps us decide what serves us and what no longer serves us in our own growth and evolution. Meditation is a key tool for sharpening your discernment, and that is something you want to keep sharp! Discernment is behind every choice you make for yourself. Your ability to judge what is best for you is what makes or breaks your life. It is the difference between happy and sad, joy and misery, success and failure, and health or disease.

Meditation combines physical, mental, emotional, and spiritual work in a very practical form. There are many methods to choose from and I often think of it as the quintessential "cross-training" technique. Through meditation, the seeds of self-discovery are cultivated and nurtured. Once you have mastered the basics, you can open yourself up to limitless inner power and deep understanding.

A regular practice of meditation brings daily clarity and cultivates the ability to move beyond the drama and past the sea of emotion that we all experience daily. Ideally, you will come to a place of compassionate detachment where emotions can no longer knock you off your centre. In my opinion, this is one of the goals of balanced living. Meditation can get you there. It will help you attune to your natural rhythms, and as this happens, you will see and experience many changes. Spend some time with your soul, stop the drama, still the inner chatter, figure out who you are and what you really want, and then draw yourself a positive map to get there. That is what I did and how I came to know true happiness and contentment. Meditation was the key to this success for me. If I can do it, anyone can! The following stories are some examples from my own life that helped me to recognize where my intuition was working and growing. These in turn helped me to develop the confidence and trust that are essential to successfully working intuitively.

## A Story Of Divine Discernment

Life is funny, is it not? We ask the universe for things and we get what it is we *think* we want, and inevitably we are tested about it all. I sometimes feel that I am a perpetual child learning to ride a bike and I experience the stage where I am getting used to not having my training wheels on. Falling off and getting back on; falling and getting back on. There was a period of about three years from when I began to officially do tarot readings professionally to when I put away my tarot cards for good in terms of using them in readings. I still teach others how to

## 6. CULTIVATE THE GURU IN YOU

use them from time to time and will still use them for myself, but I basically stopped offering those readings as a professional service.

I am not sure why, but those few years were chalk full of odd experiences. All useful of course in terms of lesson learning on my part, but odd, nonetheless. It was a strange time in my personal and intuitive development. By day, I was this mainstream corporate person crunching numbers and making product decisions in a completely non-spiritual environment. At night and on weekends, I spent my time pursuing my spiritual path and doing psychic readings. For a time, I truly felt like I was living a double life.

I met a lot of unique characters during this period of my life. One time I was invited to a small spiritual fair as a vendor. So off I went with my bag of tricks, my cards and candles and incense. I really do not know why I went to these events as I did not particularly enjoy them, and I eventually became resentful as I had a full-time job and began to feel like I was squandering my free time. My "friend" wanted me there though for some reason, so we could do things together, so off I went.

I set up my working space and sat waiting for someone interested in a reading. This particular time, two odd things were happening simultaneously. One, there was a man across the room staring at me for hours. He would stare at me, then walk by and pretend that he had not been staring. This was a small venue so it is not like this would go unnoticed. Every attempt that I made at contact was met with aversion.

Frankly, I did not care. For me, this whole psychic gig had never been about money since I had a *career* in marketing. Yes, I was still telling myself that at this point. I just carried on and figured he was a bit of an odd duck. Other people however noticed too. They began to comment. As you do at these things, like any trade show really, you circulate when you do not have a taker at your booth. As I amused myself by circulating a bit, I was being told things about this man. "Oh, I see you have a friend there," one would say. "Watch out for that one," another would say. I was amazed. I imagined that there were probably some jokes out there about how many psychics it takes to change a light bulb. These people could not mind their own business if their lives depended on it.

While all this went on, there was another person, this time a woman, who came to my attention. She was rather elderly, and I thought she looked to be of Caribbean or Jamaican descent. She was one of those people who was tiny in stature, but you just knew she was mighty in every other way. She came to my attention specifically because she began circling me in a rather obvious way. Again, it was a small venue. The first two laps went pretty much unnoticed but then she began chanting something and that all changed. She stopped then, boldly standing beside me, staring directly at me, assessing. Things became a bit uncomfortable and then downright weird. Then she just bolted back across the room to her spot. She beckoned me over.

The intrigue was getting a little too much for me, but I tried to remain pleasant. As I came to stand in front of her, she pulled her glasses down on her nose and stared into my eyes for a good while. She then gave me the biggest smile, her rickety teeth adding to her charm and the twinkle in her eye, and then she spoke. I was not prepared to hear a Welsh accent come out of that woman and that made me laugh with joy. "Strong," she said. "Strong, strong, strong. You are the strongest I have seen." I really did not know what to say to this, so I just smiled and said, "Thank you." Then she turned and walked away.

## 6. CULTIVATE THE GURU IN YOU

Back across the floor, I had a customer waiting so off I went to do my thing. When that had finished, the room had pretty much cleared out. I began to shut down and pack away my things and as I turned back to my table, the staring man was suddenly in my chair. He wanted a reading. "Just my luck," I thought, but hey, this is what I was here for, so we proceeded.

"I have been watching you," he said. "I noticed," I said. "I waited until the others had all left," he said. "OK," I replied, and then I just did a reading for him.

He was basically a nice guy who was pretty caught up in his ego and an unhealthy relationship. He had begun to dabble in some of the "dark arts" as they say. I am a pretty laidback person, so I did not respond to all his dark energy mumbo-jumbo. I just spoke to him like a normal person. I commented that it did not look to me like it was making him all that happy and I suggested that he maybe give all this a miss for a while and concentrate on the people and things that did make him happy.

Something happened then. He dropped his guard, relaxed, and actually smiled. He told me that he really was interested in something completely different. I suggested he be kind to himself and try some meditation. He told me that I was not like the other people there and I replied that indeed I was not.

Later I asked the coordinator of the event if they knew who the Welsh lady was, since I did not get her name and wanted to track her down. She told me that she had no idea who I was talking about and that no lady like that had been there as a vendor and she was pretty sure that she had not seen anyone come in like that for any services either. Since it was such a small engagement, she was quite certain.

She asked me then if I would be willing to come there every Saturday and do readings from that space. I declined. To this day, I am not sure what that was all about, but I did get some wonderful Divine insight. I knew that the psychic reading circuit was not for me and that my time in that New Age world was coming to an end. I had come to the conclusion that New Age and what I knew to be spiritual were very different things. I knew that I would never fear people deemed to be "dark" or negative. I never did. Deep down they are just like everyone else, people dealing with wounds and insecurities. I also knew that maybe, just maybe, Angels can show up as little old Welsh ladies.

I truly believe that my years of meditation are the foundation and strength that underpin my discernment, and that discernment is what has allowed me to successfully navigate the challenges in my life. My foundation of meditation has allowed me to develop intuitively and psychically in a balanced way leading to my professional success as a medium.

On the heels of that adventurous day, when I decided to no longer do psychic fairs, I was invited to go to a company that was setting itself up to do on-line readings. Yes, the age of the internet was blowing up the airwaves and the psychics were getting in on it. At the previous event, I had met a girl who had really liked me at her reading, and she had asked me to come along and meet some people that she was working for who were setting up a new venture. Lucky me, I thought.

I headed out to this "interview". I was to take a small test and then do a mini reading for her boss. I packed up my kit once again and was off on yet another psychic adventure. I thought, this is what I was supposed to be doing, right? I approached a warehouse which was the address that I had been given. I have to say it felt a bit sketchy to me from the outset, but I did not

## 6. CULTIVATE THE GURU IN YOU

want to be too judgmental. After all, what did I know about the internet business?

I was shown in by the girl whom I had met at the fair and walked through the length of a huge space to an office. As we walked, I saw several cubicles set up. That was where the psychics were going to work from, I was told. I passed another bunch of larger little rooms that had plastic sheeting covering the openings. It was all a little weird. I was introduced to a manager who, while friendly enough, was also a little hyper and looked as if he were jumping out of his skin. I thought immediately it could be drugs. Again weird, but I just went with it. My intuitive senses were highly charged however, and I was feeling dubious by this time. The whole scene seemed a bit combustible.

I was ushered into an office which, to my utter relief, seemed totally normal. Here I met my acquaintance's female boss. She seemed pleasant enough and very professional. She reviewed with me how the interview was to progress and took me to a little desk area where I could do the first part, the test. It was like a little spiritual quiz, kind of cute really. There were some questions about tarot cards, numerology, and astrological signs. The kind of thing that assesses your general knowledge of New Age things. It took me less than 10 minutes and oddly she seemed impressed by that. The next part was her mini reading. This wasn't a big deal for me, and she seemed genuinely happy with it and said she would likely be booking a full session with me. I was then taken to a waiting room of sorts while things were discussed with the higher-ups.

Before long, she returned all smiles. I was deemed to be just what they were looking for. Yay me! Then it was time to get down to the nitty gritty of how things worked. I was given scheduling information and a basic run down of the operations and the expansion plans of the business. Then it was time to talk cash. I sat back listening to how it was all to work out, because let's face it, business is business. If I was meant to spend an hour commuting and was taking on shifts on top of my day job, you can bet I was expecting to be paid for my work.

I was informed that the readers were going to be paid $12.00 an hour. Now at the time the minimum wage where I lived was something like $7.50 an hour so I guess that they thought that was quite a good deal. "Ok," I responded. "And what are you charging?" I asked. Well clearly, she was not prepared for that question. "A dollar per minute," she replied. "So, let me understand you. You are making $60 an hour and I am making $12 an hour and I am doing all the work." She really was not expecting that. "I may be psychic, but I can do math. Sorry but I don't think so. Thank you but I do not think this is for me." Off I went.

I did get a call later from them offering me $20 an hour but I trusted my intuitive vibes and respectfully declined. I later learned that they had been busted by Vice for cocaine trafficking and porn. They were connected to some not very nice organized agencies including a huge international psychic hotline.

Shortly after that I stepped away from the "New Age" crowds and stopped doing reading parties too. Instead I signed up for a six-month meditation course with a Buddhist Monk after deciding that that would be a far better use of my time. I was excited to get back on my spiritual path. Although I valued my psychic skills, I did not feel doing reading parties was the best way to cultivate them. I was so grateful for my Divine discernment through all of that, and how it helped once again to prove to me that my intuitive vibes always lead me to the right path. I trust them unfailingly and they have never led me astray. I will be forever grateful though to those people I met at that time in my life. They taught me a lot about myself and about what I did and did not want in my life.

Meditation is like anything else. For it to be effective, two things must happen. First, an internal change must occur, and you must ask yourself if you ready to try this. Second, you must act on this change of mindset and remain dedicated and open. As with anything, you get what you give. Action equals results.

So, who is meditation for, you may be asking yourself? My answer is who *isn't* meditation for? Everyone can benefit from meditation. In fact, you've likely been in a meditative state many times and just not realized it. For example, have you ever been driving home from somewhere and ended up in your driveway without really remembering the journey home? Have you ever been washing dishes and finished them without realizing that you were almost finished? Have you ever awakened from a night's sleep with the answer to a problem? These things happen because your subconscious mind is at work. This is the same sort of process that happens in meditation. Meditation is just a form of processing thought. It does not need to occur in a church, in the lotus position, or chanting "OM".

There are so many positive reasons to meditate, you will wonder why you have not already begun! Once I developed a disciplined practice, some of my standout benefits included an improved state of calm that I carried with me throughout the day and I witnessed my brain working faster and more efficiently. Tasks that would take me 45 minutes I did in 20 minutes. My energy levels went through the roof and maintained themselves throughout the day. My intuition was heightened, and my stress seemed to not have the same negative impact on my health. Things and people that usually pushed my buttons no longer had that effect on me, and in general I seemed to always be much happier as a person. My emotions were always level no matter what was happening on the outside, no more roller coaster. I felt like I knew the biggest secret to happiness that there was, and I could not understand why more people were not meditating! Just google "benefits of meditation" and you will see just how incredible it is.

It is important to also know that a regular practice of meditation at some point will take on a spiritual aspect. This does not mean that you will have a sudden desire to study astrology and listen to BoHo music. It does however mean that you may want to stay open to new experiences such as developing a deep emotional connection with yourself and ultimately to the world around you. As this happens your life will shift, and you will experience an expansion of awareness that will change you in positive ways and ultimately impact how you walk through the world.

There are many different methods, beliefs, and philosophies out there concerning meditation. It can be overwhelming to get a foothold on the subject. It is always nice to have a teacher or at least someone with experience to discuss your experiences with. I believe that once you have a few basics down, trial and error is the best way to move forward. Looking for a class or starting a group is always an option. I suggest gathering knowledge, testing that knowledge with your own experience and then making your own determinations about it.

People do ask me about the different kinds and types of meditation since there is often confusion and so much information out there. I explain it like this. There are basically

## 6. CULTIVATE THE GURU IN YOU

two types of meditation: active meditation and passive meditation. Think of your mind's power as a bank account for a moment. Understand that certain acitvities add to the bank account while other activities deduct from the bank account. If we are primarily engaging in activities that reduce our bank account, we will end up very depleted. We must engage in activities that build up the bank account, so that it is always at the ready when we need to access extra energy.

Not all activities are equal in terms of how much the currency of mind power or the energy costs. For example, all cars are not created equal and there is a range of price that that they cost. Likewise a quiet 30-minute meditation will leave you energized where as a 30-minute marathon will leave you far more energetically depleted. Certain activities cost us more energy and use up more mind power than other activities.

For example, if you engage in a 30-minute guided meditation which is usually a positive experience, it can leave you energized and even excited, but it actually costs you some energy and some mind power. It is what I call an *active* meditative exercise. Any meditation that requires you to "seek" anything, be it images, sensory feelings, messages, or insights is *active*. They all require that you "spend" from your mind's power bank. A sitting meditation however, where you simply sit and cultivate a neutral mind is a *passive* meditative exercise. *Passive* meditative exercises "add" to your mind's power bank.

While you are striving to build your intuition and your spiritual gifts, it is likely that you will be engaging in all sorts of active mind exercises. It is very important that you make time for a practice of passive meditation as well so that you can replenish the mind power that you use.

Keep in mind that different activities use different amounts of mind power. For example, if I were to do a psychic reading for someone, I would without question be using a significant amount of mind power. It would require several hours of silent meditation to replenish the mind power that I would use up in a single-hour psychic reading. Generally speaking, anything that you feel "uses up" your energy is using up some of your mind's power and anything that you feel is "giving you" energy is adding to your mind's power.

People often ask me what my "practice" is, or what type of meditation I recommend. My answer is two-fold. I always encourage a cross-training of meditation with a key foudation of silent practice. I base this on my own personal experience. I have gained tremendous benefits by engaging in all kinds of guided meditations, group meditations, distance meditations, chanting meditations, sound meditations, and creative visualization meditations. They have all provided me with different experiences and insights and they help to raise my energetic vibrations in some way.

I can honestly say that I have benefited the most from a regular practice of walking and sitting meditation that are done together. I got further in terms of intuitive and spiritual development and in reaping every day benefits with this practice than I ever did with any of the others. Because of this, it is what I most recommend to people. Once you have a solid foundation of built up mind power, it is far easier to develop intuitively and psychically. To maintain high energy levels and a high vibration, it is important to make sure that your energetic mental foundations are solid and strong.

But how do you ensure that your overall foundation becomes solid and strong, and stays that way? As always, you must begin by examining your physical, mental, emotional, spiritual components of living. Are you doing your best to ensure that each of your components are co-functioning in a healthy and balanced manner? Are you doing what is required to nurture yourself so that you are living your optimum life? Are you doing what it takes? If you are, fantastic! If you are not, then make this your place to begin.

Below are descriptions of the walking and sitting meditation practice that I use. The practice of these two techniques back-to-back have been the single most effective tool and meditation style that I have used to strengthen my foundation. For me, this has been a critical step to my expanded awareness and enhanced intuitive ability.

## <u>Intuitive Training Tip #7 – Walking & Sitting Meditation Technique</u>

With any meditation exercise, there are some general things to keep in mind. Always make yourself comfortable, but not so comfortable that you fall asleep. When possible, choose a calm and quiet environment. Try to practice at the same time each day so your body will get used to the routine and you will progress quicker. Keep your face and body relaxed and begin with some deep breaths to focus and settle yourself. I recommend setting a timer for the 15, 20, or 30-minute interval that you are choosing to use so that you know when to transition from walking to sitting meditation.

Walking meditation enhances your ability to focus and relax the mind, which will serve to both increase your energy and your vibration. At the same time, because you are moving physically, it will prevent you from falling into a trance mode. Though a trance state has its purpose and place in meditation practice, it does in fact deplete both energy and mental capacity.

Essentially you are pacing back and forth for a specific period of time, so give yourself enough room. Perhaps a hallway or across a living room. Anywhere there is a clear path where you won't hit anything. I recommend that you do this inside to avoid as many distractions as you can and can focus intently on the task at hand.

Initially you begin with reciting a simple two-syllable mantra, though eventually your mantra falls away, and this is normal. The reason for a two-syllable mantra is to match it with the in and out breath. Examples could be Hello; Amen; Believe; or I Am. Anything that suits your fancy is fine as long as it can be matched with your breath. Also, it is important for you to choose a focal point on your body. This could be your heart, your solar plexus, your throat, or your forehead, whatever feels natural and comfortable to you. This spot will evolve to be a power centre of sorts, the place from which you can harness your inner power. Proceed as follows:

- Eyes open, looking forward and down in front of you keeping your gaze a few feet ahead.

- Head and neck at a comfortable level.

- Hands crossed comfortably in front of you resting easily, one hand on top of the other.

- Begin to walk at a comfortable pace, not too slow and not too fast.

- Follow your breath and direct it to your focal point.

- Recite your mantra, mentally in your head, over and over again. If you notice you have not been saying it, just go back to it, and do not worry. It will ebb and flow naturally.

## 6. CULTIVATE THE GURU IN YOU

- Acknowledge any thoughts that come into your mind and just return to your focal point, your breath, and your mantra.

Please note that it is always best to practice walking meditation prior to sitting meditation as the first prepares the body and mind for the second. Always split whatever time you have between the two if possible. If you have only 30 minutes a day, split the time 15 minutes walking and then 15 minutes sitting. I do not recommend more than 60 minutes in total of meditation per day. Thirty minutes is all you need to reap the benefits, but do not be surprised if in time you want to go for the 60 minutes, it is that good! More time spent in meditation does not equal faster development intuitively. If you can only fit one type of meditation in, always choose walking meditation, since it is the builder.

Sitting meditations are especially important for spiritual growth once the foundational work, or building format, has been done such as after a walking meditation. The sitting meditation is where, if you choose, you can allow your mind to drift into a trance mode. A trance mode is simply the place where you can experience great feelings of joy and happiness and it can be a place where real insight is gained. You are primed by the walking meditation to connect to the subtle realms. You could connect with Spirit Guides or receive messages from your higher self, your Angels or even deceased Loved Ones. It is a place where, for a short time, you may forget that you are actually meditating. It is quite natural and nothing to be fearful about.

However, it is vital to understand that a trance mode is also where your foundation will be tested. You may experience various types of phenomena such as colours, sounds, vibrations, or voices. Only with a very strong foundation created through many hours of walking meditation and balanced living, will you be strong enough to have the mental capacity to accurately discern phenomena from true insight.

As you meditate and as your practice develops, it is likely that you will have experiences that can be felt on all levles. Some of these may include:

- A sense of warmth or cold thoughout your body.

- Dramatic heat or cold in specific areas of the body.

- Tingling sensations in limbs or top of head.

- Queasiness or nausea.

- Mild to extreme emotion.

- Floating sensations.

- Mental imagery, symbols or visions in your mind's eye.

- Sensations of colour.

It is important to try not to allow any of these things to distract you. While it can be fun and even insightful to analyze these experiences, they are merely by-products of a meditation practice and should never be the goal of your practice.

The best rule of thumb when practicing sitting meditation is to not become attached to anything that you experience. Don't worry about it and just continue to build up your foundation. When doing a sitting meditation, stay in an upright position with your back straight. Keep your feet on the floor, relaxed and with uncrossed ankles. Allow your hands to rest comfortably in your lap. Tuck your chin slightly so that you do not place undue stress on your neck. If you smile ever so slightly it will help your face muscles to relax. Take a few deep breaths to settle yourself and enjoy.

## **Quick Recap:**

One of the most important factors in developing your intuition is having a strong mental foundation. With a strong mind, you can focus, discern, and articulate effectively, efficiently, and clearly. The stronger and more developed your mind becomes, the less likely you are to get caught up in emotion. While emotions are an important element of formulating information, they can also become a distraction and impede intuitive impression and insight.

Meditation is a form of self-discipline that when practiced leads to an expansion of consciousness and a strengthening of mind power. It is about bringing your physical, mental, and emotional states into harmony, then learning to *access* and *direct* the energy that comes with that harmony. As well, it is a vehicle that provides an inward journey; a means of discovering *who* and *what* you are at the deepest possible levels.

Meditation can be practiced by anyone and has many far-reaching positive benefits. When practicing meditation, you may experience certain phenomena such as visions, temperature changes, body sensations, seeing colours, and other things. It is best to observe and take note of these things but not to get distracted by them.

There are many forms of meditation, some active and some passive. Some build your mind power, and some deplete it, so it is best to have a daily practice that builds while also experiencing types that do not. Walking and sitting meditation are an excellent way to accomplish this when they are practiced together.

# 7. FINE-TUNE THE GURU IN YOU

## 7. FINE-TUNE THE GURU IN YOU

Deciding to embrace your intuition and to develop your spiritual gifts is a big step. It will involve some big shifts in personal growth and will change how you experience and perceive the world. In my opinion, it is totally worth it, and I cannot imagine any other way to live. Yes, it is a *process* and while the concepts may seem intimidating, taking your time is important to ensure that you maintain balance in your growth and development. I believe it is true that we are never given anything more than we can handle. So, while I bring your attention to the potential changes that can occur, it is equally important to assure you that there is nothing to be nervous or anxious about. I firmly believe the intuitive path is what will lead you to living your very best life.

Fine tuning the guru in you is all about the trial and error of learned experience that can only be achieved by the *process*. Like anything else in life, it is over time that knowledge is refined and perfected. Only by learning from your experiences will you be able to apply that knowledge to everyday life and it is in this process that you come to master yourself and your life. How long it takes to learn a lesson is individual, but everyone must go through the same type of refining process, so don't ever feel like you are alone in that.

I imagine that if you were to sit and think about it, you would be able to identify for yourself certain lessons that you learned and the circumstances that led to that knowledge you gained. Working intuitively is no different. Each experience builds on the knowledge of the last so that eventually you get to a place where you deeply understand yourself. The more times you experience it, the deeper you will come to know your process in it. This all helps to build trust in the overall process, so that eventually you always know just where you are in it.

It is like going to high school as an example. At first everything is new and intimidating. After a few years, though, you know how it all works and there is a comfort level that naturally happens because you have experienced enough of it to understand its process. By the time you go on to college or university, you get another new set of experiences but you have the knowledge of having being in a somewhat similar position, and that makes it just a bit less intimidating or disorienting than before. You have sort of been there and got the t-shirt. By the time you are out looking for a first job, you have a much better understanding of yourself in new situations and so you move through that process a lot smoother. It is still new but now you have life experiences and are able to take the lessons from those and use them to navigate yourself through even more complex or different situations.

Each time you grow, your perspective shifts. How you approach, navigate and handle life also changes. This is normal. When you add intuitive knowledge to the mix, the shifts and changes take on an even deeper experience. It can make you feel more alive and connected to everything than you would feel without that intuitive awareness. Working intuitively will lead you to a sense of being divinely led or guided at times and that is an immensely powerful feeling. That is something that moves you in ways that can elevate your trust in the Universe and deepen your soul connection, even when it can seem that life is not working smoothly. In my case, as the following story will illustrate, I found I really needed my intuition at times when life is not working smoothly.

## A Story Of Divine Perspective

Between the age of twenty-eight and thirty-four, I was involved in my first serious relationship. It was during this period that I went through some of the experiences I have discussed here. I was in a very high stress job trying to navigate the corporate ladder I thought I wanted to be on, and I was experiencing what was really my psychic opening (rather than a spiritual awakening). Throughout this time, I experienced a lot of underlying emotional turmoil of a challenging romantic relationship and a tremendous amount of career pressure.

To say that it was an intense time is an underestimation on a grand scale. If ever I thought that having cancer was the most intense experience of my life, one that cracked me open, this later period in my life showed me that it had not. In fact, in many ways I came to feel the cancer chapter of my life helped me to cope with it all that was to come in my late 20s and early 30s. I had been given the gift of perspective with my cancer, and that has been like a life-long inner compass that brings me back to the North Star.

I believe the saying that love (romantic love) is stupid. The things we do and put up with because we have bought into the illusion of romantic love astounds me. It can be like an illness. It can make smart people make unwise decisions. I was no exception. Added to this, I was struggling with having the undiscovered psychic skill of an empath, and when all this collided, it was the mixing for a bad cocktail. When you love someone, and you can see the beauty of their soul shining so brightly, you can forget to measure it against their actions, and the result is soul crushing. I had to learn this lesson the hard way. But learn it I did, and I have never made that mistake again. Thank you, God, for my lessons.

This relationship began with great challenges. Here are just a few: disapproval from family; opposing cultures; little common life experience; a significant age gap; mixed families with different children from different mothers; and quite different life priorities. But we were in *love*. The *big love*, the *one*, or so I thought. To be fair, we were in love and that love was real. I know this, and thankfully I have never questioned that or felt bad about that.

The unfortunate reality was that while the love was real enough, there existed an inability for that love to be equally and freely given, and that was the imbalance that eroded the foundation of our love. I came to realize that my partner's best attempt at love, honesty, and faithfulness were not even equivalent to what I would have done as a half-assed effort, and there is not much about me that is ever half-assed, so in the end it did not work out.

It is a sad thing when you find yourself lonelier in a relationship than you know you would be without it. That was the position I found myself in five years into this relationship. Increasingly it became a situation I knew I would be unable to mend. There were other problems to be sure, such as a lack of communication, limited time together, dishonesty which I knew was there but that I could not put a finger on. I knew that a deep soulful connection was missing, and I knew I was the type of person that needed that.

## 7. FINE-TUNE THE GURU IN YOU

To make matters more difficult, I knew I was with a man who would not understand any of this. We did not fight or argue, and we genuinely enjoyed each other's company when we spent time together. Our sex life was good and healthy. We did not have any financial problems. He was self-employed, and I had a good job. I knew he would never understand it if I tried to end things because our life was good in his mind, and he would not understand what the problem was. His past was drama-filled, and we did not have any of that. So, while I believe he wanted to live a peaceful and calm life, his ego still needed the drama because to him, drama equaled desire and love.

As a couple, you know when things are bad. We became ships that pass in the night, and I did not know what to do. I did not see a way forward and I wanted to leave the relationship. I had come to learn that there were things I did not even realize that I needed and wanted in a relationship, and I knew that I would never have them if I stayed. I also knew that I wanted a child or children and that I was not with the man that I wanted to do that with. I needed some answers and some resolution.

On my way to work one morning, I was listening to a talk radio show that was featuring a psychic. I heard the DJ say, "Call in now to get an on-air message and win a reading." It was one of those moments where life stops, when you just know something big is about to happen, just like in the movies. I looked at my cell phone on the seat beside me, then back at the radio, then back to my phone. Before I knew it, I was dialing the number and I just knew I was going to get in. I did. In that moment, I was given a message that rang true about my relationship and within 10 minutes I had won and booked a full session with the psychic from the radio.

A week or so later, I went for the appointment. As I came in and sat down, this man said to me, "So, he killed you before in your last life. Are you going to let him do it again?" To say I was unnerved in that moment is an understatement. Some time prior to this, I had had an experience whereby I had a past life memory recall of that very thing he was mentioning to me. This statement really hit home, and I paid very close attention. To be honest, I do not remember anything else from that reading other than I had decided that what was required was for me to heal this karma with my partner. To accomplish this, I was going to have to leave the relationship with love, not hate or anger. It was a big revelation.

On many levels I was ready to leave that relationship right away, but the whole idea of the karmic wheel, which I believed to be true and real, made me bide my time. To be honest, it was not that hard in a practical sense since he was not really paying much attention to me anyway. I saw him briefly for only maybe two hours a day. I left early for my work and he came home late from his. I had had my radio reading in the summer, and I coasted along like this for as long as possible.

By the Fall, I was beginning to feel desperate. I hated living a lie and it became a serious strain not being honest with how I was feeling. The last thing I wanted to do was make myself ill. Too late, I did that too. I was told that I had precancerous cells in my cervix and underwent a painful procedure to have them removed, not once, but twice. This is what happens when you are not dealing with your stuff. Your body begins to tell you to pay attention and take action.

In desperation, I called the radio psychic and basically told him where I was at. I will never forget this call as long as I live. I believe it was a case of Divine Intervention. I was attending church with my parents and in an effort not to combust, I went into the church basement and called the psychic from my cell phone. He warned me not to do anything. He told me that at that moment in time, my partner was like a pressure cooker and that if I left now it would push him over the edge. He would become violent and I would pay the price for that. He told me it would all be over by January. I was unsure how I was going to possibly make it to January, but I heeded his warning and was thankful. I made sure to thank God before I left church that day.

That was in mid-October and we carried on. I was very frustrated because I was ready to leave and it's not my nature to withhold my feelings or be deceitful in any way and that was how I was starting to feel. I also knew that something was going on with him. I knew it but I did not know what and I had no evidence. I knew that my intuitive vibes were never wrong. My partner seemed to change a little bit toward the end of the year, and he suggested that we go away for New Years. We were in our sixth year together and we had never been away together. No holidays ever, not a single one. We did go away and just actually spent a weekend in a hotel room watching movies and spending time together. It was nice and it was fun, but it also made me so very sad because I knew that if he had only allowed this kind of thing to have happened more often, we might not have been in the situation we were in.

When we returned from that weekend, he began to discuss getting married. Out of the blue he wanted to go look at wedding rings. I was like, what the hell is going on? This was the furthest thing from my mind. I knew the time was coming where I was going to have to get out, things were spinning out of control. Two weeks later in mid-January, I got a strange call one evening. As I was making dinner, waiting for him to come home, I was told by a mysterious caller that my partner had been having an affair for some time and that he was the proud papa of a three-month-old girl. Everyone in the community knew but me, that they had all known for months. She went on to say that she was sick and tired of hearing her friend, who was the baby's mother, go on and on about her relationship with my partner like I did not even exist. She felt bad for me and that is why she was calling. The caller said she felt I had a right to know.

Whatever this woman's motivation for making the call, I was grateful. In that moment, I experienced Divine Grace. I was able to push the hurt and shame and embarrassment aside and realized two very important things. In an instant, I could see that this had little to do with me and everything to do with the insecurities of my partner, given who he had chosen to have the affair with. But most importantly for me in that moment, I realized that this was my ticket out of the relationship. That this was something that he would understand and accept as a proper reason to break up. In the chaos and whirlwind of emotion in that moment, I was so very grateful for the blessing of clarity that allowed me to see it, finally a clean way out. Still a bit difficult and messy, but a clean-cut way to end things.

Overnight my life became one of those crazy T.V. reality shows. I was very calm about it all. I congratulated him on his latest child as I stirred the pasta. I left his dinner for him on the table and went to bed in the spare room. I heard him on the phone later that evening obviously talking to the baby-momma and he said to her, "I really didn't need this right now you know." When I heard that I thought to myself even now he is making this all about him. Though I felt completely humiliated and betrayed, just then I also felt relieved. I was moving on. I moved out the next day taking only my clothes. Eventually I came back for the bed which had been mine before we got together, which was in the spare room. A girl needs a bed after all.

## 7. FINE-TUNE THE GURU IN YOU

For the rest of his life, he tried to get back together with me, even after he was living with someone else. He always blamed me for us not being together because I could not get over what he had done. I never got back together with him, though it did take about a year for us to fully move on. I was damn sure that I was going to ultimately leave things in a good way between us because I was sure as hell not interested in doing a dance with him like that in any future lifetimes.

I did forgive him fully and truly from my heart as I grew to understand his emotional limitations. He was a good man, but he had his weaknesses and I was able to get to a place where I did not take them personally. About five years later, he got colon cancer and died. He was only fifty-one. We were able to have a final conversation where I said all the things I felt I should have said: that I loved and forgave him.

I was able to see him one more time at his home. Hospice had sent him home to die which is what he wanted. His sister who was there told me that my timing was bad, that he had just been given his morphine and he would be out of it. Well, he was a strong-willed man. He must have heard my voice and sensed my presence because he sat up suddenly in the middle of my visit while I was at his bedside and stared boldly eyeball to eyeball with me one last time. He died the next day.

Many things happened at that funeral that were so unexpected. Of course, when I got to the church, my brother was already there and had chosen a seat. Just to be sure I had truly forgiven him, God decided to test me. Guess who was sitting literally right in front of me. The baby and the momma and didn't that baby turn around and want to be fully engaged and completely in my face. Yes, that is right, the Universe will test your convictions and to think otherwise is just being naïve.

At that funeral, I was also able to close a major chapter in my life. From many associated parties, I got the respect they had never given me before. I got compliments, adulations, and affection from a group of people who had belittled, shunned, and, in some cases, abused me. Of course, I was not looking for any of that. I cannot deny that it felt good and just and right. It was a strange day.

Looking back all these years later, I can honestly say that I am so very grateful for that crazy period of my life. It taught me so much about who I am and much of my intuitive and psychic development evolved then. I learned so much about my capacity for love and in turn for forgiveness. It was also a period where I learned the depth of my belief and trust in God and in the Universe. Much of the time I had little else to work with, just a tiny seed of knowing that it was all leading somewhere and that it was all going to be OK.

Throughout it all, despite the hell that I was living and experiencing daily, I believed and trusted that it would all work itself out. It did, though not in any way that I could have imagined. As I navigated the wreckage that followed this period, I kept my faith at the forefront of my mind. I came to trust my intuition more than anything else in life. I learned that faith is a form of love and it is one of the most important acts of self-love we can give ourselves.

During the time frame where this story took place, I really threw myself into my spiritual life. A lot had happened. I had been given ample opportunity to test my spiritual mettle and practice non-attachment. I left my home, all my belongings and drew a line under my life. I also lost my job when I was

## 7. FINE-TUNE THE GURU IN YOU

let go due to restructuring two weeks prior to leaving for Thailand on a trip of a lifetime. It was such a time of extremes. So many moments of synchronicity and Divine Intervention. So many lessons.

We have discussed that everything in the Universe is made of energy and energy is *dynamic*. By this I mean that energy has momentum, movement, it evolves, and it can be changed. Remember that you are made of energy and are affected by all the other energy that surrounds you. Life is energy interacting with energy, on all levels and realms. The better you know yourself and your inner terrain, the deeper your awareness of the subtle realms will be. Learn to pay attention to those intuitive nudges. They are always right and are always trying to tell you something. Things are not always how they first appear. Being able to decipher subtle energy, subtle information, and use it to your advantage is the purpose of developing intuitively and of fine-tuning the guru in you.

Everything is propelled by energetic momentum and can be altered if you are aware of it and learn to work with it consciously. If your personal awareness of how energy is working in your life is sharp and focused, everything will take on new depth and meaning. Engaging your body, mind, and soul, as well as working consciously with your intuition, will lead you to a new way of being alive and experiencing life. So many times, I would have been lost if it were not for the knowledge I received intuitively. Acting on those tidbits of information helped me to clear the path forward for myself and helped clear emotional and karmic debris.

Whenever you find yourself in flux it is important to check in with yourself often. Keeping balance in life is so crucial to successful intuitive work, it is critical to remember to check on that balance as if it were your bank account. Remember too, that this means checking in on all levels, physical, mental, emotional, and spiritual. It is so important to always reassess your intentions along the way and to check that your ego has not got you off track in any way. Remember we are all works in progress!

Re-evaluation is a constant thing, a normal thing, and a crucial thing. If you are not yielding the results you think you should be in any area of your life, I suggest you step back and reassess. It is likely that some unrealistic expectations or attachments have snuck their way into your mental view and emotional process, and that your ego is at play. I believe a process of re-evaluation is necessary to create a fertile neutral mind, an open and compassionate heart, and the correct energy for successful and sustained intuitive work.

## **Intuitive Training Tip #8 – Taking Stock Intuitively**

Grab a notebook and pen and settle yourself in a quiet comfortable place.

Divide a page into four spaces, one each for physical, mental, emotional, and spiritual.

Take a couple of minutes to set the tone for some personal intuitive work by closing your eyes gently, placing your hands on your heart, and taking a few long deep breaths. Tune into your body and your mind, and to how you are feeling. Just simply observe where you are at. If you are not feeling relaxed and calm, keep taking slow deep breaths until you settle and feel *tuned in*.

Think about all the aspects of your life as they pertain to the four categories on the page. Ask yourself if there is any place that you feel things are not working in a way that you want them to be.

## 7. FINE-TUNE THE GURU IN YOU

Where is there something that you are not happy with? What things or relationships are not feeling as positive or smooth as you might want them to be? Just ponder things in a general way.

When you feel ready, begin to jot down any of the things that came to mind in their relevant category. When you have exhausted all the things that came to mind, turn the page to begin on a clean sheet of paper.

Take each point in the individual categories one by one and expand on them. Include what you feel solutions might be, and how you can take responsibility for your part in each point you have listed. See each situation in your mind and ask yourself how it makes you feel. What do you instinctively sense or feel about it and about your role in it? As you connect to your soul, to your intuitive side, ask yourself what to do about it and write the answer down. Perhaps you need to change how you are perceiving things? Perhaps you need to take some action? Perhaps you need to talk to the other people involved? What ever it is, ask and then write down the information that comes.

Examine your answers. How do they make you feel? Now spend some time creating an action plan to help shift where the current situations are. What actual things do you need to do to get things where you want them to be?

## Quick Recap:

Embarking on a path to cultivate your intuition will ultimately have a ripple effect on your life. It will in time increase your awareness and this will provoke change in how you perceive and experience life. These changes will spur personal growth and shifts in your life energetically, and possibly personally and professionally as well.

It is normal to feel uncertain about things as you grow and change. All of this is part of a larger process. It will take some trial and error to hone your intuitive skills. As discussed, everything in the Universe is made of energy. Energy is *dynamic* which means it can be changed. The more aware and sensitive you become to energy, particularly subtle energy, the more you will become aware of your intuitive skills and the ability to energetically enhance your life.

You experience energy at your physical, mental, emotional, and spiritual levels. There is no separation between these levels, they all work together. You cannot experience something on one level without it impacting all the levels. The deeper you know yourself, the more consistent your intuitive impulses will become. You will begin to refine your skills and sharpen your sensitivities.

As you proceed in your intuitive work and development, it is important to check in with yourself often and take stock to make sure that you are in a balanced place physically, mentally, emotionally, and spiritually. It is more important to be sure that your intentions are aligned with your soul rather than with your ego. You will find that listening to your higher intuitive and spiritual-self more often, works out much better than following your selfish ego-centric self. If you do this and keep in check, you will see your world transform before your eyes in all the best possible ways.

# 8. INTEGRATING THE GURU IN YOU

# 8. INTEGRATING THE GURU IN YOU

This is the time to dive in and start really connecting with your intuitive side. As you go about this and start to gain more and more daily experience, you should know that there are certain considerations and preparations to be mindful of. It is important to prepare yourself for intuitive work, just like you would before a test or an interview or that kind of thing. You want to ensure that you always get the best results possible from your intuitive efforts.

When you are preparing for meditation, or setting out to work with some oracle cards or other divining methods, or even just tuning into your higher self or connecting to your Guides or Angels, there are both internal and external preparations to consider. Learning how to deal with negative energy will become equally important. This type of energy work, for that is what it truly is, will yield certain results and experiences. Learning to manage all of that is just as important as developing and expanding your intuitive skills.

Depending on where you are and what you are planning to do, there are some basic qualities and mindsets to put into place before you begin any active intuitive work. These are what I refer to as *internal preparations* for intuitive development.

Some of these are qualities that you may want to embrace in your everyday life as you begin to engage with and cultivate a relationship with your intuitive mind and the active energy that comes with that type of work.

Firstly, ensure that your approach and your intentions are aligned with your spiritual self and with higher spiritual consciousness. By this I mean take some time to check in with yourself and make sure that your head and heart are synced. Are your intentions for this work of the highest kind, for the betterment of yourself and for your higher purpose? Second, you need to check in with yourself to make sure that you have a neutral and open mind, devoid of expectation and attachment. Are you feeling positive and not overly emotional about anything? Make sure that you are not physically, mentally, or emotionally distracted by something other than what you want to immediately focus upon.

Then you need to move your inner awareness and conscious mind into your spiritual heart centre to ensure that you are working from a place of soul connection. Your intuition is in fact the voice of your soul. Your mind and brain are just your operating and processing system, and sometimes they can muddle the communication, so it is important to have an inner soul connection before you begin all intuitive work. So again, take some time now to be still within your mind. Prepare yourself, your inner landscape, as if you were going to meditate. Quiet the chatter in your mind. Connect with your breath and settle your physical body. Quiet yourself on all levels and connect with your inner self as deeply as you can. Become peaceful and calm within yourself. Give yourself time to get there and just observe your process. This will become more and more effortless and natural the more you practice.

## 8. INTEGRATING THE GURU IN YOU

Equally, it is important to check that your physical environment is conducive to getting the best results possible. These are what I refer to as *external preparations*. Are you in the right physical condition to be doing this work? Are you energized and relaxed or are you tired with low energy, or too wound up and hyper? Consider your clothing; is it appropriate and comfortable, or is it constricting? Are you wearing something made from natural fibers or synthetic ones? Do your best to make sure that you are in a calming, clean, quiet, and inviting space that compliments the sacred work that you want to engage with. Does the décor resonate with your vibration and give you the feeling of expansion or contraction? Consider all these things.

How have you set the stage for your work? Have you considered the temperature, the colour, and the light? Are you using incense, music, or a candle? Are the electronics off if your space? Have you allotted the appropriate time and set up the appropriate boundaries so that you do not feel rushed or distracted? Are you hungry or too full? Is your body rested and ready? Have you got the appropriate props to see that your needs are covered such as a comfortable chair or cushion, a blanket, or some water?

This may all sound a bit much, but really all these things are important and can impact the success of your effort, especially when you are just beginning to develop. Remember you are impacted by everything in your orbit. It is just like going to sleep. We all sleep better in a certain environment, right? This is the exact same principle. Take the time to set yourself up for the most successful experience possible. It will make a difference and can help or hinder you on your learning path.

Your mind is your most powerful ally along with your faith. Your mind can lift you to heights or drag you down low. Your faith can bring you hope when all seems lost and give you the confidence to move mountains, while lack of it in yourself or anything else can make you want to hide from life. Your mind and your faith are therefore the most important elements to consider when doing intuitive or energy work of any kind. Remember that energy follows thought. Thus, how you approach the topic of negative energy will completely determine your experience of it. Examine your core beliefs around what you are doing in any area of your life. They will dictate how you experience everything.

Your belief system is based upon the accumulation of verbal and non-verbal suggestions that have been gathered throughout your life experiences. Through patterns of repetition, their associated rewards, and disappointments, we learn to create our own perception of reality. You therefore become what you think. The power of the mind is an incredible thing, and your thoughts truly do create your reality.

If you believe that everyone and everything is of a Divine and eternal energy, then as such, you cannot be vulnerable. If you feel that you need protection, then you do not honestly believe yourself to be Divine. Those two thoughts are mutually exclusive; they cannot be held at the same time. I always approach *negativity* of anything as merely a lack of light. We know that light can diminish under certain circumstances, certainly, but I do not believe it ever ceases to exist. We can illuminate the darkness with our divine light just like a flashlight illuminates a dark space.

If you believe or embrace fear in any way, including with just a thought, it will close you down and block your connection with your intuition and with spirit. You will become ungrounded and not centered, and your ability to discern will go out the window faster than you can imagine. Your energy, thoughts, and

## 8. INTEGRATING THE GURU IN YOU

experiences will all mirror your fears. The key to minimizing the potential for fear to take hold is to be well grounded, with balanced energy. Ensuring that you have taken care of all of your internal and external preparations will help do this, as will practice.

Become an unshakable force and back it up by an unshakable faith, a faith which trusts and knows that the powers of Spirit and the Universe have got your back. It is that simple. Get to this place and you will grow in every way that you want to, providing your ego and intention are in balance and are alignment with your soul. When you have that in place, surrender it all to Divine timing. Remember the world of energy is your natural world.

Therefore, the power of your mind and the strength of your light are all you need to face any *feelings* of negativity. If you make this your core belief, nothing else will be necessary. If you "feel" better by adding in some sort of protection for yourself before undertaking intuitive work, or anytime you are not feeling quite right, then do so with the power and conviction of your energy. Know and trust that you can handle every situation with the power and strength of your mind and spirit. Call to your Angels and Guides to receive help with awakening this within you. If things seem complex now, know that as time passes and your experience grows, and as you integrate the guru in you, it will all become very natural and easy.

Engaging in intuitive work will obviously create many changes for you as your energy and vibration begin to change and elevate. You will likely feel these changes physically, mentally, emotionally, and spiritually. You may feel at times that you are on a rollercoaster ride or even jumping realities. In some ways, you will feel your own energy change and shift along the intuitive path. Just try to keep your faith in check and do not rush your work. Let the process unfold naturally for yourself.

Changes and challenges will soon pass as you integrate new higher frequencies and energetic rhythms.

Here are some potential things that you could experience:

- Physically: Headaches; migraines; off centre or dizzy spells; flu-like symptoms; tiredness or spurts of great energy; feeling outside of yourself; nausea; bladder/bowel responses; new or odd pains; perfect health; sleep interruption; deep sleep; or busy dreams.

- Emotionally/Mentally: fear; anger; anxiety; confusion; excitement; motivation; sabotage; denial; guilt; ego; peace; bliss; love; ignited mind; or compassionate detachment.

- Spiritually: lack of faith or increased faith; trust issues; doubt; spiritual elation; increased hope; excitement; or deeper connection to nature and to the universe.

Always use your common sense and if any symptom persists for more than what seems a reasonable time consult your doctor. More often than not however after a few days you will notice the intensity begin to dissipate as the energy shifts and your new vibration settles in. Sometimes it's obvious and other times it's subtle. The more experienced you become at working intuitively, the more familiar you will become with detecting energy shifts. You will notice things quicker and eventually they will not seem so disruptive. The frequency too will lessen the more expert you become at integrating your energetic shifts and assimilating vibrational changes.

Learning to navigate all of this may seem overwhelming. I can assure it is nothing to feel anxious about. Think of all the commonsense things you should be doing to take good care

## 8. INTEGRATING THE GURU IN YOU

of yourself anyway. These are the things that will also help with integration as you develop and change. Add into that meditation and contemplative activities, as well as getting in touch with nature as often as you can. These will help to ground and center you. Consider increasing your water intake, eating a clean nutritionally-sound diet, and adding in gentle movement like walking, stretching, or yoga. Anything that will help you to have body-mind-soul awareness in a calm and balanced way will help you manage better. You may notice you require more rest and sleep. This this is normal. Allow yourself to give into what your body is telling you that it needs, and what your soul is directing you to do. Try not to think about it too much, rather just surrender to the process and act with awareness and dedication to your path.

We are not given a human manual for navigating life. Generally, we must figure it out as we go along. Developing your intuition is very much the same, however the better you get at it, the more you feel as if you are getting the upper hand. It is as if you have the inside scoop that other people are missing. Yet it is here for all of us.

The best decisions I have made in life have been completely intuitively led. They enabled me to grow in amazing ways both personally and professionally. Most of the time I truly had no clue why I was taking the actions I found myself taking, other than I had allowed my intuitive insights to lead me. I know how crazy that sounds, but over the years I have proved it to myself again and again. So many times, that now to act intuitively is just like breathing for me. In fact, I believe I have actually forgotten how not to live intuitively. It is just my way of living and how I walk through life. It is who and what I am. My life absolutely got better once I learned how to surrender and trust my intuitive messages and stopped resisting.

# A STORY OF DIVINE TRUST

One day in meditation, I was given the strangest message. When I meditate, I generally am not doing so to gain any specific information or insight. I just show up, follow my breath, and get into my meditative groove. Sometimes it happens that I receive messages. This day I did receive a message that made no sense. I mean I got it to a point, there was some logic to it. Essentially though my response was, "Why would I do that?"

At the time, I was working in a good steady job that had little stress and afforded me the opportunity to gain ground financially as well as the mental freedom to focus on my business. By this time, I had been facilitating spiritually based workshops and classes as well as teaching yoga classes for several years. As clear as day I received the message to go and become a Nutritionist. I can tell you that nothing could have been further from my mind. My guides told me that this was the missing component to my business. I already covered the mental, emotional, and spiritual aspects and I needed to add in the physical. I argued. I explained to the Universe that I teach yoga and that is physical. They replied, not like this will be. I was not convinced in any way, however my past experiences had taught me that my guides were never wrong and that though I did not understand this now, there would certainly be a reason that I was being guided to do it. So, I investigated.

I have always loved learning, so I was not opposed to going to school. The cost was hefty, but I had always been interested in health and in nutritional topics so I also knew that it would be interesting, and I am a firm believer that any education is a good thing. I decided to go for it and was able to go down to part-time hours at my job. I figured I would also have more time to build my clientele and to work on courses. I would soon come

## 8. INTEGRATING THE GURU IN YOU

to learn that there were many reasons indeed why I got this message and I will be forever grateful that I listened and acted.

It was not long into my new program that I started to notice people were watching me, much to my chagrin. I had decided that I was going to attend and keep my mouth shut; just get in and get out and not really get too involved with things beyond my course curriculum. I was not going to tell anyone that was a medium or psychic. Well, I guess the Angels had a good giggle about that one because I think it was in my third class that the teacher looked at me funny as I was leaving and said, "You, what is it about you? There is something different about you."

I quickly came to learn that if you are going to surround yourself with people who have actually done a lot of personal work and have good mind-body-soul awareness, the chances are good you will run into some pretty intuitive people. So, there I was, outed. In an odd coincidence, a fellow student who happened to lag behind and catch all this piped in and had a question about her deceased grandmother which I was able to help with. Funny how that happens.

A few more weeks went by and I was in a business class. Having had a professional career in marketing, I quickly saw that this course was sorely outdated. I could not let this go since I was paying for it after all, and soon I was in the manager's office pushing for changes.

Before I even graduated from this program, which I thoroughly loved, I became a facilitator for the college. Upon graduation I began teaching the business course. I also was asked to create a continuing education course on the body-mind-soul aspects relating to having a client-based business in nutrition. For a few years, I did this and was given some fantastic opportunities to meet and work with amazing people, people who were really some of the most aware and spiritual people I have ever met and been connected to. I travelled across the country teaching my course and I feel I helped create awareness among practitioners to consider the role psycho-spiritual influences more deeply have when working with their nutrition clients.

From the outside, I know it looked like I was well on my way to having a successful business in that field. It was all going swimmingly until one day, at my biggest event to date, I stood at the podium after the lunch break and I was about to begin the second half of the day's presentation. As I stood there looking out at all the wonderful eager and engaged faces, I knew this was the last thing I wanted to be doing with my life. I knew that this was not for me and this was not where I wanted to be and that this was, in fact, not my path.

You can imagine that a multitude of feelings began to flood in. I carried on well enough with the day, but a cascade of thought and confusion began to weigh heavily upon me. I began to back out of opportunities. I felt disheartened and confused and a bit fraudulent beyond that point because I knew it was not working. I kept asking over and over in my mind, "What was the point of all this?" I had spent so much time and money investing in this path, and I had enjoyed myself for the most part.

As I fell into a pattern of working at my part-time job and doing my business still, I reflected heavily on the past two years. I came to see that all along, there was a part of me that was forcing the energy, wanting to love it all because it was manifesting and I thought that I should be loving it all, since I was making it happen.

I realized that deep down, there had always been something that was not quite right for me. I realized that it had all taken too much effort beyond what something you love should take. I did not wake up and jump out of bed excited to practice as a nutritionist. It did not really jazz me. As much as I wanted it all to be my thing, it just was not. I really believed that it had been what I wanted, to teach and to lecture and to be engaged with people that way, in a way that helped and made a difference. I knew so many people that wanted to have what I had and wanted to do what I was doing, and here I was with it and did not want it. What was wrong with me?

This certainly left me in a pickle. Things were pretty rough for me then. I felt like I was just going through the motions on so many levels. I felt like a fraud. Even on paper, it wasn't looking good. I was 41 and I had two part-time jobs that were not really going anywhere. I was still single and having no luck meeting anyone significant. I was feeling more and more suffocated in my town, where I had lived for 30 years. I knew something needed to change, but what? I began to toss around all sorts of ideas in my mind. One giant thing that was holding me back was the fact that my parents, whom I was living with at the time were getting older. They were in their eighties and their finances were a mess and they relied heavily upon me financially and otherwise. I knew that if I decided to move away, they would have no choice but to sell the house. They would have to move far away from their friends and from their church, which was a huge deal for them. Life was intense.

A good friend of mine had moved about two hours away to a town that I had been to several times throughout my life. One weekend a few of us decided to go and visit her. One thing I can gratefully say is that God blessed me with wonderful friends. They have truly been the nectar of my life and in this department, I have been truly blessed. So off we went for a girl's weekend, which with my friends always means there would be some spiritual activities involved along with great food and great talks.

For some reason I was behaving in a way that must have seemed very anti-social, which was highly unlike me. I kept getting the nudge from Spirit to walk and walk alone. There is a beautiful river that runs through her town and it kept beckoning me. So, time and time again, I went to walk. One of these times I was resting, staring out into the water and I heard *the voice*. Allow me to explain. As I have mentioned here, I often connect with my spirit guides. I have also had experiences with angels and other beings in Spirit. Of the voices that I have had experiences with psychically and as a medium, there is one voice that is unmistakable. It is a voice that is above all voices. I have only heard it twice in my life thus far. The only thing I can compare it to is in the movie, *The Ten Commandments* with Charlton Heston when Moses is on the mountain at the burning bush.

The voice said to me "You must move here." I looked up and in my mind's voice, I said, "Why would I do that?" "Because your energy is needed here," came the reply. I thought about this for a minute. I understood this to some degree. I know what I do as a medium, and I know what energy I bring with me to a place. Still, I thought, that is a big ask. I have no job here. I don't know a single person here besides my friend who had just told us she was moving away. I had no family here and not a single professional contact. So, I put all this to the voice. The reply was unmistakable: "You need to move here to meet your husband." That made me gasp out loud. I had always wanted a husband, and that is something that I had never told anyone. That was *big*. That was a bigger deal than I have ever admitted to anyone. The use of that specific word for me was the biggest hook the Universe could have used to get compliance. I was officially unnerved.

## 8. INTEGRATING THE GURU IN YOU

I returned to the house where my friends were, but I did not utter a word of this experience. I immediately began looking at real-estate in the area. There was another location that I had been leaning toward relocating to and my girlfriend made an off-handed remark about blackflies, which illuminated the last reason *not* to move to this town. My unnerved feelings settled in deeply. I did not sleep that night and was out early in the morning walking again, this time with a different view to the scenery.

Two months, later I came back for a solo visit. My girlfriend was packing and planning her move back to our town and I told her my story. "Well, you have to move, that's all there is to it," she said. She is a very matter of fact person. I knew she was right. I felt it in my bones.

Still this was the hardest decision I have ever had to make. I knew this would wreak havoc on my parents and force them into a situation that was the last thing they needed at 82. I had been in that situation with them for a decade now however and a little piece of my soul was dying each day because of it. It was time to move forward with my life. I determined to tell them, even if it meant that I would become the black sheep of the family. Even if it meant I walked away with nothing except my cat and a knapsack of stuff to the new town and got a job waitressing. I would just focus on the first step and worry about all the rest as it came. The burden of what I must do felt heavy but for the first time in a very very long time, I felt a glimmer of hope and a bit of excitement for myself and for my life.

A few months later, I sat my parents down and told them of my plans. I made sure to build in enough time for them to do what they needed to do in a way they felt comfortable with. I was in no rush now that I had a plan. They were in shock as I had expected. In some ways, this forced them to look at the reality of their own situation and my father had quite a history of being an ostrich, so he was not happy about being forced to look at things. I forged onward and explained myself and my situation and laid the whole plan out before them. They said that they wanted a few days to think about it.

I had felt so very guilty even though I had nothing to be guilty about. I realized then that this was a karmic thing for me with them. Putting myself first for once was breaking a karmic pattern for me and that is why the whole thing was so difficult and such a burden. Deep down I knew it was the right thing and I intuitively knew that this was going to open up my whole life. Three days later, my parents came to me and told me that they wanted to come with me. It was to be their last adventure and they were looking forward to it all. Now it was my turn to be shocked. I can honestly say that this scenario never once crossed my mind. *Ever.*

Although it was like pushing an elephant up a mountain to make this move happen, I knew it was also Divinely led. In a matter of three months, we moved into the best house we all ever lived in. The synchronicities were remarkable. We listed our current house, a friend's parents bought it, I found a new house online and that was that, we were moved. Me, my elderly parents and my cat, we all moved to a new place where none of us knew a soul or had any experience. It was indeed an adventure. Divine trust can be a scary thing to navigate, but in my experience, it is always warranted.

As you become practiced at living more intuitively, your ego driven need to know why everything in life is unfolding the way

## 8. INTEGRATING THE GURU IN YOU

it is will settle and diminish. You will find that you spend less of your mental and emotional time and energy in a place of worry or anxiety. The unknown elements of your life will cause you less and less concern. It will feel weird at first for a bit perhaps, but then it will just feel great. A sense of trust in the process of life will weave into your consciousness and it will change your perspective on things and your approach to the world unfolding around you. As your growth and experience integrates, you will experience a new sense of peace and inner happiness. Not because a specific event has occurred, but more likely because of a new-found belief in your own ability to successfully move through your own life. You will start to feel that your pulse is on the energy of things and that you can make better decisions because of that. It will bring forth a new confidence within you and a new respect for the energetic world around you.

## **Intuitive Training Tip #9 – Infinite Being Meditation**

Once again, settle yourself into a state of receptivity by taking some deep breaths and creating the appropriate inner and outer environment to do some active intuitive work. Read through this exercise first and then try it for yourself as a meditation. It may also be useful to record yourself reading this script and meditate to a playback of it. Be open to whatever information presents itself, however it presents to you. Remember that you may see, hear, feel, or sense information in any way or even in multiple ways. Whichever way you get your information is perfect. There is no right or wrong way. Be sure to make some notes afterwards so that you can be reminded of your experience later.

Settle into your inner mind and inner sanctuary. Allow your body to relax and your brain to quiet. Take as much time for this as you need. Imagine yourself as an infinite being of light and energy. Sense the expansion of you. Sense your energy growing and expanding to fill up the entire room or space where you are. Experience that in any way that feels right for you. Familiarize yourself with your process of expanding your energy, and your awareness of that energy.

When you feel comfortable with that, expand yourself once again. Imagine and sense that you are now far above and beyond the town where you are at. Sense and feel that expansion. Breathe deeply into yourself. Sense yourself extending and expanding energetically. Now imagine taking your energetic self out into the atmosphere, high above the planet. Feel how amazing it is to be so energetically free and above it all. Sense your personal power and control of all that you are. Sense yourself being at one with the Cosmos. Feel the limitless of your being and the strength of your energy. Feel your power to make thigs happen for yourself.

You are an infinite being of light. You have all choice in how you direct your energy and your will. You have the power to instantly change perspective and how you experience life, just like you can control and expand yourself energetically. You have this power. You are this power. You are an infinite being of power, energy, and light. Remember this and remember who you truly are.

In your own time, come back to your breath. Feel and wiggle your fingers and toes. Take a moment to reflect on your experience. When you are ready open your eyes and make note of anything you feel is important.

## **Quick Recap:**

As you begin to make living more intuitively part of your daily experience, remember that it is important to prepare yourself for the times that you engage in doing your intuitive development work. Considerations like internal and external preparations are important. Some of these include making sure your intentions are aligned with your spiritual self and that you keep a neutral and open mind. Your environment too needs to support your intuitive work so be mindful of the space you are in, the clothing you are wearing, and the state of your physical body. Remember that experiencing physical, mental, emotional, and spiritual changes as a result of developing your intuitive and spiritual skills is perfectly normal and just part of the process. There is nothing to feel anxious or worry about. It's all good.

The power of your mind and thoughts, as well as your deepest core beliefs, will create the reality of your experience. This is especially true when dealing with negative energy, which is a natural part of life. How you approach it will determine how you experience it, so keep that in mind. Use common sense in terms of taking care of yourself as well as getting enough rest, fresh air, hydration, and proper nutrition. These actions will all help you manage the changes that you will experience as your intuitive skills begin to blossom.

# 9. EXPAND THE GURU IN YOU

## 9. EXPAND THE GURU IN YOU

Now that you know that developing your intuition is a process, it is also important to understand that that process has a deeply *creative* element to it. I do not mean creative in an arts and craft sense, but rather in a sense of creative energy which cultivates growth. As you develop your intuitive skills, new and different aspects of your intuition will unfold. There is somewhat of a domino effect that happens. Along the way, there are different tools and techniques that will assist in your intuitive progress. It is like going to the gym. Different machines help to define and build different muscles. The same goes with your intuition and your spiritual gifts. With the right workout, you can optimize your intuitive muscles and expand the guru in you.

Visualization is one of these things. You will have practiced a bit if you have done some of the exercises in this book thus far. It is an excellent tool and one I encourage you to spend time working with and developing for many reasons. It is a key part of the intuitive process. Visualization is a technique that uses pictures or imagery and engages the imagination. Your brain is divided into two sides: the left logical side and the right creative side. Most of your life is spent using the left logical side of the brain. By yielding to our right brain, we access the mind-body connection which restores balance in the brain and opens us up to change and renewal. This balance within the brain helps with the natural development and healing processes of the mind and body.

Visualization uses imagery to change your emotions. It causes changes to your feelings, which then turns into a physical sensation that can open talents, glean insights, relieve stress, or even reduce symptoms. It has been proven that negative emotions lower our immune system and keep us bogged down mentally. Having negative emotions tends to delay and even prevent us from reaching our goals and inhibit the brain from accomplishing what we want. Positive emotions, however, boost the immune system and make the brain work in a balanced mode that is more conducive to change.

When you begin to actively utilize creative visualization, you open yourself to all the magic and bounty that the Universe holds for you. Visualizing is something that people do every day. It is just another, more active, way of using your imagination. When you visualize, you are essentially using the same techniques that you use when you imagine something. For example, when you were a child in school and the teacher asked you to pretend that you were a tree or a bunny rabbit, you used creative visualization. Whenever you visualize something in your mind you are taking the imagination to another level. You are taking an idea, picturing it in your mind's eye, and actively trying to manifest it in your physical existence.

Energy follows thought, therefore when you imagine or visualize something, you are putting universal and personal momentum and energy behind it, driving it to manifest and become reality. Thus, you must be careful with your thoughts and energy and consciously try to have a positive focus. One of the things to remember when you begin to visualize and meditate is that, because energy follows thought, it is vital that your intentions be sincere.

If you practice with an open mind and a willingness to change, grow, and learn, you will soon find that your visualizations are becoming experiences. For example, if there is a relationship or a situation that is causing you some difficulty and you practice visualizing it working in a positive, nice, flowing manner, eventually you will see it begin to change. We can create anything we want in life, and at the very least, we can control the effects that our environment has on us and the effects the people around us have on us.

In my experience there are two types of visualization. The first is very simple and most like using your imagination. It is *creative visualization*. The second type is where we begin to move toward active meditating instead of passive, and that one is more of an *intuitive visualization*. This second one involves aligning yourself with soul's energy and the natural principles of the Universe and learning to use these principles in the most conscious and creative way possible.

For the sake of argument, let us agree that we are all here in this world to work on our spiritual development. We do this by moving through our lives, learning, and growing from all our experiences. This is our process and it is a completely individual thing. Our spiritual development is equally individual, and very much an internal process. As we proceed through our lives and experience our world, we are all influenced by certain ruling principles that govern our world. Theses ruling principles are known as Universal Laws. I will expand on these principles and the Universal Laws in the following chapter. For now, to simplify, know that when you experience struggle in your life, it is safe to assume that you are in some way going against one of the Laws. When life seems to be flowing easily, know that you are in sync with the Laws. In my life I have learned that it is always easier to flow with the stream than against it. Learning to work with the Universal Laws makes it a lot easier.

It does not always follow that flowing with the stream is necessarily perceived to be easier in the moment, as the following story will illustrate. In some ways this is where creative visualization can really be an asset, a tool to help you rise above life's challenges. For years I had visualized my ideal home. I believe I did this both consciously and unconsciously. Every time I was exposed to something that made me feel a certain way, such as a piece of furniture, a garden, the set or scene of a movie, if it gave me a certain vibe I worked it into what I envisioned to be my perfect home. I kept on doing this regardless of life's challenges that often made me think I would never be able to get what I wanted, or never be able to afford it, I kept the vibe alive.

This type of thing happened from when I was very young, long before I knew what visualization was. I could just close my eyes and see it in my mind's eye, the type of home I felt I was meant to be in. I could feel it so deeply that it became like a living breathing thing. For years and years, I had always been drawn to antiques and to the Victorian era. Everything about that time just resonated with me and felt very familiar and natural. I am sure I had a past life in that time. I often would feel out of place because I was not living where I felt I should be, in the type of home and town that felt right to my being.

Understanding now that energy follows thought, can you imagine the volume and momentum of energy that built up behind this vision over the years? In the end, without even consciously trying, I manifested my exact home, in the exact type of setting, in the exact type of town. Imagine what you could do if you spent time visualizing consciously in a detailed and directed way? Always remember that energy follows thought and energy is what makes things happen in life. When you take responsibility for your thoughts and your energy, you can manifest your deepest desires in spite of any challenges you may face. Never give up on your dreams or what feels intuitively right for you, even if you can't see how it might happen.

## A Story Of Divine Surrender

Isn't it interesting how life always tests your conviction? Moving to the place I now live required a huge leap of faith. I had left everyone and everything I knew behind to start over. It had been one of the hardest and most challenging things I had ever done. When I arrived here, I thought, "Finally, I did it." I had always visualized myself living in a stone Victorian house and now I was!

I was naive to think that arriving here was the end of the challenges. I learned that part of taking a leap of faith sometimes includes having your spiritual mettle tested, and then tested again. In fact, it can mean enduring several tests. When you tell the Universe that you are ready for big changes, be prepared to be thoroughly tested.

The move to our new home happened during a three-day snowstorm. It was a nightmare. By the time the movers arrived (five hours late), they were beyond caring about our possessions and just threw things willy-nilly randomly throughout the house and in the yard, and as I discovered later, several items remained undelivered. I was at the delivery side of things alone and found myself in a house with eight angry, sketchy men whom I know if I had not been holding half of their money in cash, I would likely have not ever seen them arrive. I sat very quietly keeping my mouth shut while they chucked my dishes and treasures about without care because I felt scared and completely vulnerable. Many lessons were learned that day.

The move also happened less than a week before Christmas, which while not the biggest problem in and of itself, led to more challenges. There were no service men working and so we went without a stove, a telephone, television, or internet. I was undeterred and plugged in an old radio and got to work unpacking, making sure there was a space set up for my parents to use as a lounge. In the early hours of New Year's Day, I awoke with a start sitting upright in bed. I had a sinking feeling in the pit of my stomach. I quietly searched throughout the house sure something was wrong.

As I descended the stairs to the cellar, my nerves peaked. I turned on the light and from the top of the stairs, I saw a piece of paper float by, and then another and another. There was enough water in that cellar to happily float a canoe, and the water was rising quickly.

It turned out that my disgruntled movers had packed the basement to the gills with a lot of things that did not belong in a cellar. I flew into action and with strength I did not know I possessed I began to hurl boxes of books and household items up those stairs as fast as I could. It took several hours work and I rescued what I could. We also did not possess a telephone book and so, as you can imagine, on New Year's Day, it also took several hours to locate an emergency plumber.

Later that morning I began to survey the damage. Some of the pieces of floating paper that I had grabbed had begun to dry.

## 9. EXPAND THE GURU IN YOU

I soon recognized them as notes from my nutrition reference material, and then from my reiki training. As I pawed through the sopping material and waded with my rubber boots through the cellar, I began to collect damaged items. It turned out that the last 15 years of my writing, research, and course materials that I had gathered and created were ruined. They all lay together in heaps of bleeding ink, completely lost. Most of this was not on a saved computer disk, so it was lost forever.

I sat in the room that was to be my office staring out the window, frankly devastated. That work represented so much of me, my past as well as the future I was about to embark upon. I was exhausted physically, mentally, and emotionally. Spiritually I felt broken. Such loss. Things I knew I could never get back or recreate. I recall staring out the window up to heaven and thinking, "What is this? What is the message here?"

I began to question everything. Had I made a terrible mistake following my intuition and my guided messages by moving here? Was this all going to be a disaster and be all my fault? Self-doubt raced mercilessly through my mind. It was all too much. I was beside myself and to make it worse, I had to keep a brave and positive face on for my parents so they would not feel any more stress or upset.

It took about three hours of meditation and contemplation before I began to get some insight. I realized that this was a bold sign that it was time for me to forge new ways of working and doing things. The idea was not to recreate what I had done before, but to create something new. It was time to let go of the past and to push myself in new and better ways. I was not happy about the harshness of the lesson, but I conceded that if I had all my old material, I would have likely just kept riding on it and not challenged myself in new ways. Still, it was a hard lesson.

Several days later and more than $12,000 in damages, we had a dry cellar once again. I tried to stay positive. The week that followed seemed to see things moving along. We now had our stove hooked up, we had cable, telephone, and internet, all working smoothly, and the insurance adjusters had visited, and things were being financially covered. I was starting to feel better and starting to mentally explore new ways that I could create some business for myself.

Less than a week after the flood, just as we were getting on track, a giant icicle fell off the roof and knocked out our telephone, cable, and internet connection. "Really?" I said to the Universe. I guess I needed to take a closer look at the theme of communication in my life. The following week, our furnace died, and we were without heat for two days. By this time, I just took it in my stride. "Well, I guess we know what we are doing with the insurance money," I said to my father.

As the months ticked by, things got better. We all got back on track and spent our time setting up our home and learning about the new area we lived in. The overall mood became far cheerier. As summer rolled in and my savings rolled out, I knew it was time to look for work. My business was limited as I did not know anyone yet, so I knew I had to start cultivating some connections. In the meantime though, I thought I had better get a job. At this point I was still travelling a couple of weekends back to the city to teach at the college, but as I worked through the winter, I knew that was not sustainable. It was really a lot of effort for not a lot of pay, and it was not making much sense to continue.

Before too long, I landed an interview in a marketing position with a well-known theatre company. As I drove to the interview, I found myself conflicted. I was quite happy and content with how things were unfolding in my life. I had made some friends and found a group of like-minded holistic people who were into the same sort of spiritual things that I was. I knew I need an income though and even though I knew that it was only a matter of time before local people would find out about my readings, I felt a bit panicked about money. Necessity had forced me to start doing telephone readings and to my delight and surprise, they seemed to work well for me. I knew that my existing clientele would eventually get comfortable with that. Still I figured, I had better play it safe and get a job.

As I sat in the interview, I answered the questions put to me and I noticed my emotions were all over the place. I felt patronized by the manager on what job they wanted me to do because it did not resemble too closely what was advertised. I quickly sensed an air of snobbery and exclusivity dripping off them and I wondered to myself if they could hear themselves speaking. This really did not bode well, as I know myself very well, and I could foresee a time where I would possibly tell them to take their job and shove it.

Did I really want to go through the exercise of all this for a few pay cheques? Did I really want to put myself in a job I did not want to be in? This was all beginning to feel very familiar to me. The simple answer was no, I did not. So, in the middle of an interview that was going very well, I stopped it. I stood up and thanked them for their time and told them thank you very much, but this is not for me. I did not want to waste any more of anyone's time, and I left. The shock on their faces was priceless. I do not suppose anyone had ever felt anything less than privileged to work there.

As I drove home, I felt a huge sense of freedom and of uncertainty. I thought a lot about why I had made the move to a new place and put myself in my current position. I realized that I had done it all because I needed a change. I did not need to recreate what I had just left and getting a job that I did not want because of financial fear was not going to get me anywhere but stuck again. I knew I did not want that.

A good friend had recently told me that, "You can't chase two rabbits and catch them both." I realized that this is what I was doing. Rather than surrender to my skills, to the fact that I was a psychic and a medium, I was trying to hedge my bets by getting a job for financial security.

I realized that I was making decisions that were clouded because deep down I was afraid. After being fearless and moving towns and changing my whole life, here I was still being gripped by fear. I recognized that this meant that I did not really and truly trust the Universe. I did not fully believe in the skills and gifts God had given me. I did not trust in my faith. I realized that was not who I was. I realized that I needed to embrace my trust and so I fell backwards into Divine Surrender. I believed and I knew that I would be supported and taken care of. I have been.

## Intuitive Training Tip #10 – Creative Visualization Exercise

Here is a creative visualization exercise for you to try. Read it through completely first and then try it. You will be amazed at how effective it is and it will help you to understand more deeply how energy follows thought and how significantly your thoughts can affect you.

## 9. EXPAND THE GURU IN YOU

Start by imagining a bowl of lemons sitting on your kitchen counter. See it in your mind's eye. Imagine that you pick one of these lemons up. In your mind's eye, imagine everything you can about this lemon: its shinny waxy yellow colour; its smooth feel; perhaps the coolness of its skin; and the weight of it in your hand. Now I want you to imagine that you pick up a knife and cut it in half. Immediately you can sense the smell. Imagine the juice running out of it. Hold it up to your nose and smell that lemon scent. It permeates your senses. Now imagine that you hold it up to your mouth and take a big lick of that sour tangy taste. Wow!

Now even if you did not try this as a creative visualization exercise, I bet that just reading these words got your taste buds going and that right now your mouth has more saliva in it than it did a minute ago. Am I right?

This little exercise demonstrates how powerful thought is, how by connecting your mind to your thought you can create an actual physical response. Energy follows thought. Thoughts are things and they create our physical reality. Know this and keep it in your awareness and your life will change.

Now it's your turn to do the exercise with your eyes closed. Be aware of all you are sensing with as much vivid detail as possible. As before, it may be useful to record this for yourself and use the playback as an audio guide to the exercise.

I mentioned above how the practice of visualization will ultimately create a domino effect as your intuitive gifts blossom and unfold, and how all of this makes it a creative process. Once you engage your imagination actively in the creative visualization process and your intuition further develops, it will unfold to the place where you begin to get psychic impressions and spiritual insights or messages. This is the beginning of the opening of your third eye, the psychic centre in all of us. With further work, this is what can lead to the unfurling of spiritual gifts such as energy healing, mediumship, and clairvoyance. It will lead to expanding the guru in you.

## **Quick Recap:**

Developing your intuition is a creative process whereby you learn to actively engage your imagination as a tool used in creative visualization. In learning to do this, you will help to advance your intuitive skills. Practicing creative visualization techniques will provide opportunities that will lead to an enhancement of your spiritual gifts. These enhancements may lead to receiving psychic imprints and things like energy healing and mediumship.

Each intuitive skill builds on the one before. This creative energy fuels the development of the intuition and all related intuitive talents. When you decide to formally embrace a study of the intuitive arts, which is what all of this is, you will experience change and growth in all areas of your life.

Be confident in your ability to develop. Practice often with the various intuitive development tips in this book and you will see results. As you become adept at understanding and knowing yourself better, your intuitive relationship with yourself will deepen. You will notice that life improves. You will begin to experience an enhancement of your life as if you were seeing it through a new lens. Instagram will have nothing on your new filter. The more you listen to yourself and trust your intuitive vibes, the less you will move from a place of fear and uncertainty. There are Universal Laws that we are all subservient to, and as you learn about them, you will see that they can help you create your perfect life.

# 10. DEEPEN THE GURU IN YOU

## 10. DEEPEN THE GURU IN YOU

Now, it is time to dig a little deeper. It is time to challenge yourself, and to be open to some wider, broader concepts that may or may not be new to you. It is time to begin trusting yourself and your intuitive process. Previously I mentioned Universal Laws and principles. Perhaps you have not heard of these before, not everyone has. We all, however, are impacted by them. It is time to begin understanding how the Universe is constructed energetically and to learn how to use that knowledge for your own benefit.

This chapter will briefly outline some of the more well-known and relevant Universal Laws for your immediate purpose as they relate to intuitive development. Always seek out more information if something interests you. I encourage you to embrace and learn about the Universal Laws and their influencing principles. As you grow intuitively, such knowledge will help to hone and ramp up your intuitive energy. It will help you become more adept at things like manifesting and help you to navigate life decisions in a savvier way so that you experience more successes than ever before.

Learning about these Laws as well as being able to recognize how you can work in unison with them, will help to limit the amount of resistance you create for yourself and hence the suffering you experience. Anything that brings about bad or negative feelings such as suffering, anguish, pain, or distress, happens because in some way, you are going against the Laws. Quite simply, when you are experiencing anything negative at all, that is your sign to recognize that you are going against a Law. Once you begin to understand the Laws and apply their principles to your actions, you can begin to manifest an easier and better life for yourself. When you work within the Universal Laws, life flows effortlessly and functions efficiently. There is no resistance and thus minimal suffering.

I know, it all sounds so straightforward and simple. However, we are human and thus are flawed. The good news, however, is that you can learn about how all this works and practice. You can choose to move more and more in the flow of life and the flow of the Laws. I encourage you to spend some time researching this, and I have suggested some materials at the end of the book for reference. In the meantime, here are a few of what I believe are the key Universal Laws to begin working with. Try to understand how they might apply to you personally.

The Universe is energy. As discussed, all matter is made up of energy, some is very dense, and some is very light. All things in form are just energy in various densities at various vibrations. It then follows that we are all part of one great energy source and thus are connected to it. There truly is no separation from each other, so remember what affects *you* affects *all*. What you can do that improves Universal energy will have a positive ripple effect on the whole Universe and everything in it.

Like attracts like. Energy is magnetic and as a magnetic force, it will attract like energy. Thus, if you put forth positive energy, you will attract positive energy. Likewise, if you put forth negative energy, you will attract negative energy. That is why when beginning to meditate, it is so important to have a clear mind and a pure intention. After all, it is really in your own best interest. Also, in your life, begin to examine what things you are happy with or dissatisfied with. What comes to you naturally and easily? What type of people do you seem to attract? All of this comes down to this simple universal law of like attracts like.

Energy follows thought. This we have discussed in length. Remember *thought* is a very light form of energy and because of this, its ability to manifest quickly is great. Nothing in life is created without the seed of thought. Everything begins in thought form and because of this, each thought is like a blueprint of something to be manifested in the physical realm. Therefore, as you begin to become a serious student of energy, you will become keenly aware of every thought you make and the results each thought yields. Once you grasp the impact of energy in the world, you must become responsible for the part you play in affecting its energy.

The law of radiation and attraction basically means *what goes around comes around*. Simply put, you will reap what you sow in life, so practice awareness as you work and move throughout your life. As well, it should be noted that there is a connected law to this and that is the law of *Three-Fold*. If you put out a negative active thought toward someone or something, that same negativity will come back to you in the power of three – three times as harsh as the original thought. Now that is something to think about!

The principle of intent is a critical component of all meditation, manifesting, and energy work. Intent can be broken down into three areas: desire, belief, and acceptance.

It is important that you truly *desire* that which you are visualizing or wanting to create and manifest; that you genuinely want it, with a strong sense of purpose and with all your heart and soul. And that you want said thing for the right reasons. This desire must be of a positive energy and vibration and must have integrity. It must not be coming from a needy or desperate place.

Part of this integrity is a true *belief* that what you desire is attainable and can truly happen. The more certain you are of this, the more likely your chances of attainment will be. You must also be willing to *accept* that which you are seeking. You have heard the phrase, "Be careful what you ask for?" This is very realistic and wise advice. You will always be held accountable for the things you manifest. If you are not comfortable with them once they have taken form, you have only yourself to blame.

With all the hard work that you are preparing to do, I feel it is important to discuss the Manifesting Principle. After all, I imagine since you are still reading that you are wanting to manifest your intuitive gifts and become open to your soul's potential. There is a real process to be aware of regardless of what it is you are trying to manifest. If you can perfect this process, the world will open to you personally and professionally regardless of what you do now or what your ambitions are.

You will notice some recurring themes in this manifestation process. They are just as important here as in previous contexts where they have been mentioned. We have all heard many times people talk about the ability to manifest their dreams and desires. Obviously, this is easier said than done. It's not like this

## 10. DEEPEN THE GURU IN YOU

is something you learned as a child, like lacing up your shoes or riding a bike. You may wonder, is there a formula? Are there directions? Did you miss something?

Certainly, in society, we can easily find examples of those who see to have managed to embrace the manifesting principle and have had many successes in manifesting. Some of those are the people seem to have the *Midas Touch*. Why then is it that some people seem to excel toward their dreams while others just keep waiting for the big opportunity to come their way? What is their secret? Luckily for us there is a sort of *map* to maneuver ourselves toward manifestation. At the very least, it is a roadmap to success in so far as we can individually contribute to our own success. How good are you at reading your own map? How responsible are you willing to become for navigating your own success?

On an especially important level, manifesting is about bringing the spiritual into materialization, having become "real-ized". Examine the things in your life that you are manifesting effortlessly without even consciously trying. Somehow you believe in having those things so deeply on a subconscious level, they are just naturally showing up in your life. You have naturally become aligned energetically and are in the stream of things. That is to say, good things, things you want, are naturally flowing to you. This is how you know you are working within the Laws. That is the key to finding your map. When you are not working that hard to consciously evoke your desire, eventually what you desire will manifest seemingly without effort if you are energetically and spiritually aligned.

My own version of the manifesting process goes like this: clarity; harmony; surrender; listening; and action. I will explain each of these in turn. I suggest you work with these concepts tweaking things along the way until you find your perfect process. Trial and error are always part of the learning curve, so have fun and enjoy.

The first step, *clarity*, means getting specific about what it is you want. As specific as is humanly possible. You must see thing in your mind's eye, your inner vision. You must name this thing. You must own this thing energetically. You need to be able to feel this thing deeply inside you. This must become a passion, something that you are unwilling to live without. You need to be able to feel this thing at a *soul level*. Here is where intention is vital. You must intend what you see. In other words, you must truly desire this thing to the degree that you are willing it from the depths of your being. Focus. Engage your imagination and your energy.

Next, you must be certain that what you desire is in harmony with your higher self, your *Divine self*. You must align your will with the spiritual will of divine intelligence that runs through you; that which knows and creates what is truly best for you, for the development of your soul. I am sure many times you have witnessed someone drive themselves in the wrong direction in life, time after time, wondering why they cannot find success. This is because their ego-self is trying to do something that is not in harmony with their Divine self.

It is important to realize that you are responsible for your own success. You need to play your part as a co-creator in your life. Your dreams and desires are not just going to land in your lap without any involvement from you. The Universe just does not work that way. If you are not willing to do your part, then you do not have the right to expect manifestation to happen.

*Surrendering* yourself to the higher good is a major part of the process. The higher good *for both yourself and others* is what needs to be paramount. Detaching from an ideal expectation and outcome is also necessary. In this 24/7 society, we have become the consummate control freaks. Releasing is 100% an ego battle. This means accepting that, as an individual, you may not be capable of seeing the big picture. If you are not able to let go of control on all levels (emotional, mental, physical, spiritual) then you are completely limiting yourself to how your dreams and aspirations can be manifested. You must surrender yourself to the higher good for it to work.

Listening to yourself, I mean *really listening* to yourself, is a difficult thing to learn. In fact, to be successful at this often involves restraining your mental thinking. Becoming successful at listening to yourself is *the key* to your future health and well-being. In our society, we are conditioned from childhood to listen to what others want and expect from us. Over time, we have become less dependent on our natural instincts for survival and have lost touch with our own inner communication system.

This is one of the benefits of meditation. The greater your practice and discipline becomes, the more in tune and in touch you will be with your inner self. The greater your connection and attunement to your higher self becomes, the easier it will become to accept divine intelligence. As this process begins to flow in a more consistent and streamlined way, you will be able to utilize those insights to better your day-to-day life.

People you see who are excelling and surpassing even their wildest expectations are the people who have tapped into their Divine source and are co-creating with the Universe. When you begin to connect with your inner self and become aware of the *little voice* of your intuition, eventually trusting it and using it to guide you, your dreams and desires will begin to manifest.

*Action* is the final step on the roadway to success in manifesting and it is where many of us seem to falter. This is where it is our turn to step up to the plate and take a swing. You've determined what it is you want. You've balanced yourself emotionally, mentally, physically and spiritually. You've surrendered and given up trying to control the process. You've listened and aligned your passion with your inner knowing and higher guidance. Now what? Now, it's time for action. The blueprint is made, the plans are formulated, and now it's show time!

This is also the time when your insecurities and fears will rear their ugly heads and try to get you to throw in the towel. Know this moment will come at the beginning and keep an eye out. This is where you will be tested and challenged on all levels. Remember the first step where clarity, intention and passion play a role? Remember when you decided that this was something that your soul could not live without? Now you must be willing to walk your talk. Bite the bullet and jump into the lake headfirst. This is where it all comes together, *or not*. You can't miss any of the steps and this final one is the most crucial: taking action.

There will always be a final test of some kind to be certain that your integrity and Divine intent are still in alignment. Often, some sort of sacrifice is required to attain the dream and manifest your desire, for example commitment to meditation. It need not be anything on a large scale and could be something as simple as prioritizing your time and focus. Just be sure to review all the steps and check that the intent and truthfulness of everything involved is aligned with your Divine spiritual intention at every step of the process.

## 10. DEEPEN THE GURU IN YOU

# **A Story Of Divine Timing**

When I first bought the house in my new town, I was excited to be within walking distance of the local pub. While I have never been a big drinker or partier type, it is certainly nice to have the option of enjoying a drink and not worrying about driving home. I loved sitting in a pub and working on my projects and people watching, even if I was only having a tea. Several months later when I had moved, I was a bit annoyed to find that it was closed and up for sale. For the next year or so, I lobbied different friends who were in the service industry to buy the pub. It was a good deal really for people wanting that life and it came with rental apartments. Really, I would have loved to have friend live nearby and have a pub to hang out in. It just did not happen though.

A year or so later the pub reopened, and eventually I made my way there. I had made one good friend in town and we decided to meet up there after the Christmas holidays to catch up. We were the only customers there, besides the owner and one waitress. It was perfect since it was quiet and they were good sports about letting us loiter for a few hours, and the food was excellent. My friend was acquainted with the owner and when we went to leave, he came running over to give her a hug and made a joke about us being there so long. It turned into a group hug. I could tell that he was feeling quite happy and had obviously had a few drinks, and it was all incredibly good natured. Then a strange thing happened. During our group hug, I began rubbing his back in a very comforting, nurturing way. It was like my body had a mind of its own. Nobody else seemed to notice this thankfully. I however was freaking out. "What the hell was that?" I said to myself. "I don't even know that person."

I just let it go and decided that it was all a bunch of nothing and happily tried to ignore it. However, I am who I am and as a lifelong student of energy, deep down I knew that it was not nothing, that in fact, it was clearly something. It was something that at that point I was not prepared to examine deeper. Over the next few months, I became a bit of a regular over at the pub. I used to take my laptop over on a Saturday afternoon and write the lectures that I was giving at the Spiritualist Church at the time, just to escape the house and get a little time to myself. I would order a pot of tea and crack away, oblivious to my surroundings for the most part. It was good for me to get out and see people and just be somewhere outside of my four office walls. It just so happened that this fellow that owned the pub worked himself on Saturday afternoons.

As those months passed on, I began to know some people in town and began to feel more comfortable in my new surroundings. I would come out socially with my girlfriend for dinner and attend the occasional karaoke night to have a laugh. As I did, I had more interactions with *Mr. Pub*, and we struck up a friendship.

It seemed we had endless things to talk about or argue about. He was a good guy and we did have a fair bit in common in that we came from very similar socioeconomic backgrounds and families. We had both studied politics at university. We were both Gemini's (which was perfect as I had specifically asked God to bring me a Gemini man, but I was not ready to acknowledge this on any level whatsoever).

In other ways however, we were polar opposites. He had several bad habits. He was a drinker, a smoker, and a partier. He was the most reactionary person I had ever met, and he was ridiculously opinionated. He could be highly irritating, and he was rather judgmental. It took me a while to tell him what I did

## 10. DEEPEN THE GURU IN YOU

for a living, because I knew the kind of reaction I would get. He made me laugh however like no one ever had, and he had the most marvelous sparkle in his eyes that showed his true soul. At the end of the day, I was amused and quite taken with him, and he was intrigued and seemingly attracted. Though we both liked to play it cool, at times we were like two little kids together having tremendous fun.

While all of this was going on, strange synchronicities began to happen. I began to see him all over town. I would be coming out of the post office, he would be going in. I would look out the window of my friend's store and at that moment, he would be walking by carrying groceries. At that time, there was a song on the radio by a guy with the same name as his and it seemed to me to be on air each time I turned on the radio. There was even a marketing campaign for this same artist and every time I walked into my local coffee shop, there was his name plastered everywhere. It was very annoying. I was doing my best to avoid the signs and so appropriately the Universe responded by putting them right in front of my nose at every turn.

One day I was headed to an auction with my girlfriend and on the drive there, I received a message from my Guides. This was not uncommon but this time I was in for a surprise. In no uncertain terms, I was told, "You are going to buy something today at the auction and bring it to the man at the pub." I argued back: "No way. I barely know this man, that's not appropriate." "Oh yes, yes, you will do this. There will be a Chicago Blackhawk's item that comes up for auction and you will buy it and give it to Mr. Pub." Knowing better than to argue with the Universe or my Guides, I sat and thought, or rather stewed. I consoled myself by the fact that this was an auction with dishware, crystal, and antiques. I had nothing to worry about. Nothing like that item that would ever be at this auction. I relaxed.

Three hours into the auction, a Chicago Blackhawks jersey came up for bid. I felt sick. "Are you freaking kidding me?" I thought. Now this was truly an ugly jersey, pretty crappy, and I rationalized that it would be embarrassing to present this to him, so I let it go. Forty-five minutes later, a new block of jerseys came up. I surrendered and bought one. For the whole two-hour drive home, I was tormented by what had to come next. I was mortified. Somehow, I now had to figure out how to get this hockey jersey to him in a way that did not make me seem like a crazy ass stalker weirdo.

It was times like this that I hated being a student of the Universe. I had to devise a plan that would allow me to save face. I decided that I would write a note explaining that this jersey came my way at an auction and that I thought he might put it in frame and hang it as decoration in the pub, no big deal. I decided that I would drop it off with one of the waitresses at a time that I knew he was not working. Perfect. I congratulated myself on being very clever. And then that song came on the radio again.

The next day, Sunday, was the day to execute my well-thought-out plan. I carefully wrote it all out in what I thought was an easy to understand note. I whipped on my walking gear, sneakers, yoga pants, and a baseball cap, and headed to the pub. "I will just sneak in the back door and leave it on the counter," I told myself. As I snuck into the backdoor, guess who I almost ran into coming out of the kitchen? Yes, that's right, Mr. Pub was there in the flesh right when he was not supposed to be. And there I was with a bag in my hand completely unprepared.

He was his usual friendly self, big smile, and welcoming disposition. And he looked good. Really good. "Hey hi," he said. Then he looked at what I was holding. "Oh, you bought me a present?" Can you say *awkward?* I was mortified and dying of pure embarrassment. "It's OK," I thought, "He will just read the card." Well no, he was like a kid. He dove right into the bag and then felt something soft. "You bought me clothes," he quipped with a scared freaked-out look in his eye. Well, I couldn't bear it any longer. I flew into a wild verbal explanation of what was on the card, like a messy word salad, explanations being tossed everywhere. I hightailed it out of there in seconds flat.

Eventually I got over that embarrassment and we continued to cross paths. He very kindly did not bring it up. We fell into a routine of seeing each other on the nights he had to work. As our friendship deepened and we began to truly know one another, it became obvious that there was potentially more than a platonic thing going on. I brought one of my best friends to the pub one night meet him and covertly suss out the situation. I had been single for an exceptionally long time, nearly fifteen years, and all my friends were really wanting me to meet *the one*. I told her that I thought I had met someone and so she was excited.

We went to the pub for dinner and operation check him out began. He was in fine form that night. It seemed his party had begun long before we showed up. Her initial reaction was, "This guy? This is the one you told me about?" She was less than impressed, but at the same time she knows me well and knew I would not have even mentioned him at all if there wasn't something of value to it, so she patiently sat and observed throughout the evening. When we arrived home several hours later, she said "I get it." "You do?" I asked hopefully. "Yes," she said. "I get it. He gets your brain. You guys have the same brain. I totally get it." She got it. That made me very happy and feeling very hopeful.

Mr. Pub and I just celebrated our seventh year together, have gotten engaged, and have plans to soon be married. While there is much more to the story and many more synchronicities I could share, know that this situation and subsequent relationship tested everything I have been putting into practice my whole spiritual life. Navigating it all took bucket loads of trust and surrender, and it had to unfold in its own time.

At the end of the day, to get what I had longed for my whole adult life took putting my fears on the back seat, letting go, and trusting the Universe and God completely. I had to take actions that were far outside my comfort zone. My spiritual mettle was put to the test like no other time in my life, but in the end, I proved to myself that listening and trusting myself did the trick. I had to put my gut feelings above what all others might say or think, and it led me to a deeper knowing and happiness.

I learned to trust myself and my intuition above all, and I know that that listening and acting on my intuition will never lead me wrong. I am eternally grateful for that, and for Mr. Pub. I once had an experience of deep insight. I was not even thinking about it, but as my head hit the pillow one night what came to me was that I wanted a man with three things: depth of character; illumination of spirit; and zest for life. Several years later, I got what I asked for, and his star sign was even a Gemini, which I had also asked for specifically, so I would get his brain, because I too am a Gemini.

The process of manifesting can be both obvious and subtle. Sometimes it feels so straight forward, and other times it can appear to have a mystical element to it. When you are in the midst of it, it can be hard to see the process in its working stages of Natural Law and their reigning principles, including the stages of manifesting. That elusiveness I feel is inherent to the process and why it is worthwhile to learn, study, and practice.

During this time in my life, I know beyond a shadow of a doubt that if I had not had the energetic training that I have, I would have had a much more difficult time navigating the unfolding of my relationship with Mr. Pub. I had to love myself enough to give it a chance. I had to allow it to unfold without falling into attachment to an outcome. I had to take action and then step back and allow him to go through his process without manipulating or influencing him. I never would have been able to ebb and flow with his need for patience and tolerance. I never would have been able to surrender to Divine timing in the way I did. I never would have been able to have held up my confidence and trust during the nearly two years it took to unfold. Time and time again, I checked myself to make sure that I was adhering to the processes and principles laid out earlier in this chapter.

Perhaps all the lessons of my life had been training for the courtship with Mr. Pub, who knows? I do believe that my ability to navigate what was presented to me so successfully came about because of my understanding of how the Universe is constructed and how it works energetically. That understanding is due to a deep knowledge of the Universal Laws and principles that I have spent many years studying. I believe that understanding, plus my meditation practice, is what has led to my personal success and happiness in life.

## **Intuitive Training Tip #11 – Practice Your Manifesting Skills**

Before you set your mind to manifesting something specific, spend some time reflecting on a few times where you achieved something amazing, something that you were really aiming to do. For example, maybe you wanted a good grade or a promotion, and you worked really hard to make it happen and it did.

Then spend some time reflecting on something that was totally awesome that happened for you that was unexpected or that you really did not consciously try to make happen. For example, perhaps you got an unexpected refund or won a prize.

Finally, spend some time reflecting on a time where you tried everything in your power to make something happen that you really wanted to happen, and you just could not make it work for you. For example, maybe you tried to win a romantic relationship that did not work out, or maybe you tried to win a spot on a team. Something that you really wanted, and it just did not happen, in spite of your efforts.

You may want to journal this exercise for yourself or your own reference. It is totally up to you. When you have spent some significant time in thought about all of this, go back over each situation again. This time try to see where some of the natural laws and principles may have been at play. Examine the sequence of manifesting and see if you unknowingly were doing the right things and maybe where you fell short.

So, let's assume you have decided to give it a try and are going to join in the manifesting game. I say game only to suggest that this can be a fun thing. I recommend early on that you try to make it fun. Start with small things. Maybe try to manifest an extra $20 this month for example. That could be finding the money in an old coat, a small lottery win if you buy tickets, or even a savings of that amount on an item you purchase. Out of the blue a friend could repay borrowed money, or you could find it in the street. Be open to however the manifestation presents itself.

Now in the next week or so, find something small to practice with. It could be like the example above, a money thing. It could be a free cup of coffee. It could be a positive conversation with someone who is often difficult. Start small and apply what you know. Keep trying. Keep testing yourself. As you go through different scenarios, examine your application of your knowledge at each stage of the manifesting process. Keep testing and trying until you prove to yourself it works, and then begin to make it work for yourself over and over again.

## **Quick Recap:**

Your efforts through body-mind-soul work will aid the cultivation of your spiritual and intuitive gifts which can be used to help cultivate your inner guidance. This will help you and in time could be useful in helping others. Remember that the role of body-mind-soul work cannot be undervalued. It is the very thing that will lead to the development of your spiritual awareness and the honing of your psychic skills.

Your mind is used as both an instrument for perception and a vehicle for reception. Your clarity and how you experience life, as well as how accurately and successfully you receive spiritual insight, is all determined by the inner and outer harmony you create for yourself. You are a co-creator in your life along with the Universe. As such, you have the ability to manifest the life you want. The degree with which you do this successfully is directly linked to the level of responsibility you take for your own happiness, health, and spiritual development.

By learning about the Universal Laws and applying their principles to your life, you can greatly enhance your happiness and your ability to navigate life decisions more efficiently and effectively. As you do this, your intuitive skills will heighten and sharpen, becoming an indispensable aid that will provide you with a special means to getting what you want out of life. The process of manifesting has a specific protocol that includes the steps of clarity, honesty, surrender, listening, and taking action. As you begin to practice and know these protocols, you will see how to create a happiness and success in life that you have yet to experience. There will be a lot of trial and error in that process and it has a learning curve to be sure. However, I know that if you stick with it you will never regret the time that you have invested in deepening your relationship with yourself and the energetic world around you. Remember that you are part of the Universe, energetically there is no disconnection to it. Its Laws are your laws. Its natural order is your natural order. Learn how it all works and you will be able to make it work for you.

# 11. LOVE THE GURU IN YOU

## 11. LOVE THE GURU IN YOU

I know, it's a lot to take in. This getting balanced and happy is hard work, and all you wanted to do was start working with your intuition. It is so important to remember that this is *not an all or nothing* situation. We are all works in progress. The aim here is to help you become super confident in your intuitive abilities. The key to excelling intuitively and even psychically is being able to come from a healthy, balanced place so that as you work, you can discern information as accurately as possible. You may have heard the expression that a workman is only as good as his tools? Well, in intuitive work, the tool is you! Your results are directly connected to the state of your physical, mental, emotional, and spiritual health. That is why all of this is so important.

As you work intuitively and develop those muscles and instincts, you will experience personal growth along the way. Your understanding of who you are and how you connect and communicate with the world around you will change. Your awareness of energy and the subtle realms will grow stronger. This will happen all the time and will keep on happening for as long as you want it to and as long as you invite that growth into your life. You will continue to grow as long as you are willing to do the work.

Keep things simple and love yourself along the way. Remember that certain actions will move you toward the balance you seek, and others will move you further from it. Just remember that desire, will, intention, and action will move you forwards and towards balance. Resistance, fear, and avoidance move will you backwards and away from balance. All movement requires actions and all actions have consequences. You get to choose which way to move, and therefore you are totally responsible for where you are at.

So now that you may have identified some areas of your life that could use a little bit of attention and work, how do you approach that? How do you ensure you have a strong and sustainable balance in your life?

To achieve balance in life, psychological, physiological, and spiritual principles must be harmonized and to do that, they must be honoured. It is only when this is being cultivated that the fertile ground for true health and happiness can begin to flourish. We were born and designed in a state of natural balance. As with all things in nature, to truly thrive in life, you must honour that fundamental principle. The deeper you know yourself, the more you align with your true nature. An arrow can only hit a bullseye when perfect alignment is present. The same concept holds true in life. If you invest in becoming aligned with your *true* self, you will hit the bullseye every time.

It seems to me that most people spend more time planning a vacation than they do planning their life. Yet, in order to move forward with confidence and health, creating a calm and happy life, both clarity and courage are necessary. That takes some thought, some reflection, and some planning. Here are the things that will ensure that you thrive in a balanced way: take time for individual self-reflection; share your life with a partner, family or friends; become involved in social and community

## 11. LOVE THE GURU IN YOU

activities; develop your professional passion; nurture your soul; and take care of your physical health.

Life integrity for me is a path of *integration*. It is about placing yourself in the middle of your life and bringing your work, family, friends, finances and so on toward unity, rather than thinking of them as separate entities. Cultivating life integrity will address the feelings of desperation that can come from trying to juggle and balance all parts of your life as if they were separate things. Remember, there is no separation.

Claiming all parts and remaining whole is the way forward as well as really examining what that means to you. What is your definition of total health and balance? The personal life integrity you need to make that happen is the first step to that destination. Life after all is the most important journey that you will ever take. Doesn't it make sense to plan well for that trip?

There is always some turbulence when we travel, otherwise we would never learn how to improve our travelling skills, so plan for it and expect it. It does not have to be something that ruins the journey and in fact sometimes, it can make things even better! Some of my best times on vacation have been ones that were not included in the initial plan, but rather things that came up along the way and some even while I got lost!

Sometimes a lack of personal growth is stopping us from achieving our goals. Removing these obstacles means working through and eliminating negative beliefs, limiting thought patterns, physical barriers, and even relationships that may be getting in the way.

The thing to remember is that everyone has baggage to varying degrees. No one gets to travel light. There comes a time for each of us along the way to ask ourselves the hard questions. One of the keys to achieving growth with grace and ease is not to give too much mental and emotional attention to your hardships or negative experiences. Try not to become preoccupied with your *story*, rather try to learn from them, accept what you cannot change and move on. Spend time nurturing your soul, not your past. Your soul is the most important piece of luggage that you will ever carry with you. It is your most precious cargo. Love yourself and you will learn to love life.

People often comment that I seem to exude a calming energy and that when they are around me, they too feel calm and peaceful in a way they do not normally feel. People love to come into my office and home for the very same reasons. I have been asked many times what it is that I do to create this calming vibe in my life. I promise you it is nothing special. It is nothing that anyone cannot do for themselves. There is no magic here, just a consistent effort to create and ensure calm and balance in my internal and external environment. And trust me, I have times when I get off balance too, just like everyone else. As quickly as that happens though, and I catch up with myself, I get right back on top of things to reestablish my peace and calm, because I know that it serves me better and helps me to be my best self.

Here are some of the things that I do and say that help me to love the Guru in me:

- I constantly nourish and educate my mind and imagination. I am always reading books and articles and listening to podcasts or books on tape. I include fiction and non-fiction, even gardening and cooking books. I am happier and have an easier time maintaining balance when I pay attention to things that interest me as a person. So, walk, talk, listen, read, and find whatever it is that makes your soul feel nurtured and loved and do it often.

## 11. LOVE THE GURU IN YOU

- I have learned to respond only to what is being presented. This way I can mentally and emotionally deal only with what is pressing at each individual moment and I do not fall into mental multi-tasking. It is the tiny decisions of everyday life that affect our deepest sense of peace and tranquility. So, I keep things very simple for myself in my mind. This usually translates to simplicity in my external every-day life. I find I get more done and have a much easier time in life when I abandon trying to multi-task on any level.

- I listen to my heart. It helps to keep me out of my mind and into my body. I let my heart drive the bus of life more often than not. I check in with what my body wants and what my heart needs to take care of myself on a soul level. This is the self-love that nurtures me daily. When my heart feels listened to and my soul feels nurtured, then I run it past my brain and adjust if I need to. There are always practicalities of life that must be taken into consideration, but they have their place after heart and soul are looked after. I think of it as an internal team effort. It makes for a happy me. Why not try it? You will be glad you did.

- I live with complexity. I accept it. Life is complicated. I have learned to live with it, and not run from it. When you create balance and harmony, you can unify all the aspects of your life. Deal with one thing at a time and stop the drama. Learn to simplify your internal process and your external process will follow. Life can be simple. In fact, I have learned that simplicity is a mindset.

- I embrace being an individual. I am willing to go against the norm and do the things that my soul wants to do. When you let go of caring about what others will think or of personal judgments, you give yourself permission to be yourself.

- I choose work that suits my soul as well as my budget. Ask yourself if your employment or career matches what you believe to be important in life. Are they good partners?

- I am of service to others. When I reach out to others it is an acknowledgement of their importance. Everyone wants to feel they matter, that they are important and deserving of love. Sometimes the tiniest effort on our part can mean the world to someone else. Giving of yourself or your time does not have to be done in grand gestures that consume your time and energy. Sometimes just a kind word and a smile can make all the difference in someone's day. Kindness is also a service. It matters to everyone, those receiving and those giving.

- I value the simple things. I find joy in simple things. I nurture my soul every day through simple things. I have learned to find the beauty in the simplest things, because I have learned how much this nurtures my soul and helps me to maintain happiness and contentment. Everyday things like fresh flowers, pretty fabric, a clean home, feeding birds, chatting to neighbours, and all sorts of everyday simple things. Learn how your soul speaks to you through the simple things in your environment. Do you feel connected to things around you? Recall, there is *no disconnection*. Be aware of how things, people, and the community around you are affecting your soul vibe, and you theirs. It goes both ways. How are you affecting the people, pets, and things around you? Are you helping to raise their vibration? Are they helping to raise yours?

- I know my story. Discern between what is fact and what is fiction; what serves you and what no longer does. Examine your emotional and behavioral patterns and reflect on your experiences. Let go of the things, people, and places that no longer serve your soul or elevate your vibration.

## 11. LOVE THE GURU IN YOU

- I embrace my spirituality. By whatever means works for you, connect with your spirituality in a conscious and mindful way. Explore it, create it, just get connected with whatever spirituality means to you and take time each day to nurture it.

Ensuring a great journey means having the right gear. Learning how to pack appropriately so that you are ready for all kinds of weather is crucial. It is important that you have the right amount of stuff. Expertise in successful packing takes practice! Think about the road travelled thus far in your life and try to identify where you got it right and where you perhaps got it less right. Take these pearls of wisdom and bring them into this next stage of your personal path.

From conception, we receive our information through our senses, including that sixth sense of intuition. The connection is what counts. The body-mind-soul connection and all the elements that fit under those three basics headings are it. The degree to which these synergistically co-exist determines the impact that they have on one another and thus on your overall health and happiness. As you strengthen each of these elements and begin to marry and deepen their relationship with each other in a conscious way, balance will take hold and your health and happiness will flourish.

We all exist in a physical way and in a mental-emotional way. Each one of us on this planet is wired the same way. As those elements are united, we have the existence of that third element, our soul level.

It is the overlapping layer between our body and mind that is the *connection* between the two and the soul is what connects the two. It is not possible to have something happen to us on only one level. What affects one, affects all. What differs from person to person is the extent to which we function at each of these levels and the awareness we have of the connectedness of our very natures.

The better you get at knowing and feeling your own *connectedness*, the more *in balance* you will become. The more balanced you become and the more comfortable you become with being in balance, the better you will get at recognizing when you are not in balance. It will also become much easier to see when and where others are not balanced. Life will show you your imbalances through your health and through all of your relationships. If you are *willing to see* the signs, they will not be missed.

What do I mean when I say: once you get comfortable *being in balance*? Think about this. When one is used to believing on a very deep level that *dysfunction* is normal, what do you think happens when they start to rid their lives of the dysfunction? They freak out! Seriously, people often struggle with change even when that change is positive and moves them in a healthy direction. It is important to keep this in mind as you do this deep personal work. It is important to keep perspective and have realistic expectations of yourself and those around you. Remember that change and growth are part of a process. There is no timeline specific to each person and there is no right or wrong way. Everyone's process is their own. There is no room for judgment, not of others and not of yourself.

There will always be initial speed bumps along the way, initial effects of getting your shit together. Fear, anger, anxiety, confusion, denial, guilt, possible physical illness, or sabotage can all be companions for a time on this leg of the journey. These are all possible short-term effects of beginning to dig around in your personal and emotional stuff. Take heart though and know that it is necessary to get you where you want to go.

You must face these things as you work through them and work towards a higher level of personal knowledge and intuitive depth. It is normal and to be expected, so don't get thrown off when it happens. Work hard to not get sidetracked for very long, and just get back on the path. Get back to work and back moving toward even greater happiness, health, balance, and intuitive strength.

The rewards really do not compare. Eventual long-term effects of getting your shit together are amazing! Improved health – breathing, sleeping, nutrition, mental clarity and sharpness, emotional balance, and more accurate perceptions. New belief systems will naturally take hold and support you. You will experience an increased self-awareness and self-esteem, and all of this will lead to improved relationships and a richer experience of life.

Once you do the work of learning to identify and address your inner imbalances, the rest becomes so much easier. It is the ultimate act of self-love! Out of the chaos will arise clarity and a renewed joy of living that you never thought possible. Believe me that you can do this, and you are worth all the effort! *This is how to love the guru in you.*

## **A Story Of Divine Action**

Part of working with energy and working with the spiritual law, the *Law of Attraction*, is taking *inspired action*. In December 2018, I was out doing my Christmas shopping. Every year I make sure to buy myself a couple of new magazines for my

Christmas stocking to ensure that I have something interesting to flip through over the holidays. They tend to bring in special items at this time of year and I happened to pick up a couple of British magazines that I had not seen before.

Also, perhaps coincidentally, around this time I also received a strange message from my Guides. I was told that I had to start an Instagram account. This was out in left field for me because at the time, I was not involved with any social media. In fact, I avoided it like the plague. However, my life has taught me to listen to my Guides and so I created an account as directed. They had told that I was going to need to know what I was doing on Instagram later on in the year to come, so I began to play around and familiarize myself with things.

I had a very busy time over the holidays, and it wasn't until January 2019 that I got around to having a thorough look through my new magazines. I came across an article written by a young woman discussing how to work with the *Law of Attraction*. This was right up my alley, and I must admit that for her young age, she seemed to really understand what she was talking about. This was not a new subject to me at all since I had been studying this stuff for years. I was impressed. So much so that I had noticed in the article that she had a YouTube channel and so I began to watch her work and eventually follow her. I also began to follow her on Instagram. I continued to be impressed with her and the content she was sharing. As it happened, it turned out that we did some of the same things for a living. She was a life coach I was too.

Over the next two months, I continued to follow her work. She was also an author and I enjoyed her work so much, I decided that I would buy her book. I too had always felt that I would write a book. I had been facilitating workshops for many years and I knew that I had a lot of existing material that I could use.

## 11. LOVE THE GURU IN YOU

I was inspired for sure. She was amazing! I had felt that there was a shift coming in my professional life, and I could feel the energetic momentum building. Building to what exactly I had no idea, but I knew that shifts were coming my way.

I even reached out to this impressive young woman her on Instagram just to let her know that despite my being older, I was really grateful for her work since I felt it had given me a fresh approach with my own clients. She replied and I finally understood the *cool factor* of social media. I was so thrilled to be connecting with someone whom I admired and who was halfway around the world from me!

That March I had a very profound dream. In my dream, I was at a party and someone handed something to me. I was looking at it and said, "Oh what's this?" The person who had handed it to me said, "Trish, that's your book!" "How cool is that!" I replied. "It's nothing like I thought it would look like." That morning I woke up and created a website for my unwritten book, just to start the energy flowing. I'd had a title for years, and always knew that at some point I would put all that I had learned on my spiritual journey into a book, with the intention of helping other people.

I knew that people seemed to be interested in my story, since almost every day my clients asked me how I came to be a medium doing readings for people. As well, I was kind of getting tired of making and printing handouts for my courses and thought it would be so much easier to just have a book for people to refer to. The dream made me feel a little excited that perhaps the time for all that was getting closer.

The book that I ordered came in the mail also that March and as I unpackaged it something odd occurred. There are only a few times in my life that I can recall that I have had the experience where it seems like my body has a mind of its own. More likely, it was that I had an odd sensory experience like I was outside myself observing my physical moves. Either way, as I turned the book over in my hand and read who the publisher was (something I always seem to do), I ran my thumb across the name of the publisher and said to myself "That's a fun name, I wonder if they will publish my first book?" It was the strangest thing, and one of those times where you shake your head and think yourself an idiot, and then you dismiss it as quickly as it happened and get on with your day. I read and truly enjoyed the book, continuing to be impressed with this younger woman. I felt that I would really like her if ever we were to meet.

About a month or so later, I was at a hospital appointment and got a text from a friend. She seemed to feel there was some urgency about watching the latest YouTube video from the author I liked so much, but I was in no position at the time to do so, so I ignored it. Later that day I did tune in and I could not believe what I was seeing. She was putting a call out to anyone who had ever wanted to become a spiritual author. She, in conjunction with her publisher, was going to select four people to mentor as authors and then help them get published. It was a very surreal moment for me. All I had to do was submit a one or two-page proposal. If selected, I would be scheduled for a phone interview by her. If I made it through that process, I would be selected as one of the new authors. "OMG!!!" I thought.

I did not need asking twice. I think I may have been the first person to submit a proposal. It was not hard for me. I had been ready for this for years! I whipped off a proposal and included my website, and my new book website, and hoped for the best. I honestly did not know what to think, so I tried not to. I figured at least I went for it. At least I took some action and regardless of the outcome, I knew I could feel good about that.

## 11. LOVE THE GURU IN YOU

The next morning as I went into my email, there it was. An email from the woman herself! I clicked it open with nervous anticipation and was thrilled to read that I had been selected for a phone interview! I was beyond excited. The call was scheduled for a week or so later and that day I felt like I was back in school going for an audition or team tryout. I was very nervous and excited. In my mind, I kept playing it cool, telling myself that even if I was not selected, this was all great experience and how crazy was it that less than five months ago I was just seeing this woman for the first time in a magazine, and now I would be talking to her directly. Crazy town!

Part of loving yourself, and the Guru in you, is taking a chance on things and trusting that you will be able to cope regardless of the outcome. Going for something just to prove to yourself that you are capable and worthy is an excellent way to celebrate your love and confidence in yourself. Never underestimate the power of this, even if you do not succeed and even if you do not share your experience with anyone. Doing something for yourself is a great thing. Choosing to feel uncomfortable is a huge vehicle for growth. Remember that. I felt so out of my comfort zone throughout that whole episode, but I have never regretted it. The experience will give me confidence to try it again and again, and that is powerful.

On a more practical level, there are also many ways to cultivate an actual practice of self-love. This is something that I would suggest is a non-negotiable habit to form. Often, we spend a lot of our energy and time seeing to everyone else's needs than we do to our own. I think in many ways this is natural particularly in terms of supporting family and friends that we love and who are important to us.

It sounds cliché of course but it is true that the better you take care of yourself, the better you can care for others. The deeper you begin to work intuitively and energetically, the more important taking care of yourself becomes. Remember to balance on all levels: emotional, mental, physical, and spiritual. The more sensitive and empathetic you become, the more aware of keeping yourself aligned and energized you need to become. You need to do everything in your power to keep your energetic cup as full as possible so that you are the best receptor you can be! This takes planning, commitment, and dedication.

## Intuitive Training Tip #12 – Making a New Life Plan

I have a running check-list in my head that I use to measure my life against which helps me to determine if it is time for me to hit the re-set button and make a new life plan. The following exercise will help you to run through this process for yourself.

For this exercise, take a few minutes to prepare yourself for some quiet reflective work. Set an intention of clearing your body and mind as you take some deep breaths in and out to quiet and settle yourself. Place your hands together over your heart, breathe deeply, and close your eyes allowing your body-mind to balance and re-set. Take as much time as you need to. When you feel your energy is right and you are ready, work through the following questions in whatever way works best for you.

- Am I rushing to get places and get things done and getting there "just" on time?

- Is there lots of drama in my life? Does it often distract me from my plans? Do perceived crises and emergencies run rampant through my life?

## 11. LOVE THE GURU IN YOU

- Do I have elevated feelings of stress or do I not think I am stressed, yet I seem to not be able to do all the things I want to do?

- Do I have anxiety over things that seem huge, but really are not?

- Am I feeling burnt out and exhausted *all* the time?

- Do I have low energy? Am I overweight or not happy with my body?

- Do I find myself angry a lot of the time and can't really place why?

- Do I no longer take pleasure from simple things (a good meal, a chat with a friend, a walk, a good sleep)? Have I lost my zest and luster for life?

- Am I experiencing a lot of brain fog and can't seem to remember simple things?

For the next step ask yourself these questions. They may give you some clues to things that you may want to tweak for yourself.

- Am I trying to "control" things or people?

- Do I worry about what people will think?

- Am I confusing happiness with the fulfillment of a superficial desire such as shopping, eating or partying?

- Do I often insist that my way is the right way?

- Could I be rationalizing situations to hide from my fears or truths I don't want to admit?

- Has sarcasm or negativity become my standard mode of thinking or the base of my sense of humour?

- Am I becoming resentful instead of setting up proper boundaries?

- Am I living in the past or the future and not in the moment?

- Am I trying to stop change?

- Am I setting up rigid goals or beliefs that could not possibly be met?

- Am I investing in expectations for outcomes?

- Am I trying too much or too hard to fulfill my desires?

- Am I so set in my mind on how things are going to be that I have become inflexible to alternatives?

- Am I letting go of and forgiving negative emotional situations or am I holding on to them?

All these questions are going to be relevant. Any time you are feeling out of balance or unhappy come back to this exercise. Your life will always show you where you are at. Be open to seeing the signs and become proactive in calling yourself on your shit as soon as you see it. It will help you move through difficult emotions faster and with more resolution. In time, and as your intuition develops, you will become savvy at knowing when you are out of balance and why. It will get easier and easier to fix your problems, the deeper you know yourself. This is the ultimate way to love the Guru in you.

## 11. LOVE THE GURU IN YOU

# **Quick Recap:**

All aspects of yourself are always connected and impacting each other even if you do not feel it that way. Look for warning signs along the way that you may not be as balanced as you are thinking you are. Your own imbalances are likely contributing to any current dis-ease or resistance you might be experiencing. Help yourself with this recognition by assessing how you got where you are now and what decisions you made along the way. Remember that we create our reality, and if there is something in your life that you are not happy about, the first place to look to change it is within.

Embracing self-responsibility for where you are at today and where you are going in the future is the only way to ensure that you cultivate happiness and inner peace. It takes work and action so set a plan to help get yourself there and ask for help along the way when you need to. While keeping your plan in mind, be mindful of your expectations. Remain flexible on how things unfold for you.

Practice self-love along the way by taking care of yourself and by nurturing your physical, mental, emotional, and spiritual sides. Trust and believe in yourself and know that the Universe is supporting you and will meet you in co-creation if you keep doing your part. Know your worth and learn to love the Guru in you.

# 12. LIVE AS THE GURU IN YOU

## 12. LIVE AS THE GURU IN YOU

We are all ruled by attaining the basic needs in life such as food, clothing, and shelter and by all of the other things in the material world like jobs, school, finances, family, friends, and so forth. All of these elements make up our day-to-day lives. When our cycle of living is heavy and laden with responsibility and obligation, a chain of imbalance begins, even if some of these things give us joy and pleasure. Often as life takes over, we neglect ourselves in some way and we can end up spending very little time self-nurturing. I am certain most of us would like to spend more time remembering who we are, who we were, and who we want to become.

Though society often subscribes to the *all or nothing* attitude, we all know it never really works. So, what is the answer? It is not magic. Making changes that create more personal balance is what you can do for yourself. Eventually those changes become new behaviours and replace patterns that no longer serve you. The way to balance lies within you. Nobody knows you like you know yourself. As I have said before, the more time you spend getting to know yourself, the easier your life will become.

The truth is there is no easy way. It is a lot of work. However, the work needs to be done in a balanced way that nurtures and supports where you are at right *now* in your life. It needs to work with you and not in a way that causes resistance. This is how to make things truly stick and have a positive and lasting impact. Living as the Guru in You means becoming really good at figuring out where you are at, encouraging and nurturing yourself without judgement, and then making a plan to move forward. Know that it is OK to be where you are at and then spend some time getting everything you need in place to help get you where it is you want to be.

Imagine a pyramid that is divided into parts. The largest section is at the bottom and the smallest is at the very tip. Think about reprioritizing your life pyramid when you are assessing what is not working in your life. Is your life pyramid bottom heavy with the grind of the physical world? Is all that is left for your spiritual nurturing the tiny bit at the top? How is this working for you? Think about switching things up and spending more time and energy nurturing the spiritual part of your life. Think about adding in more of the things that bring you joy and that keep your energetic vibration elevated and strong. Try letting this be the biggest section of your life pyramid and see how things change.

Throughout this book, I have mentioned receiving messages and insights from Spirit and the Universe. These help to give you that extra intuitive edge as you navigate life. How can you access that extra help and direction that is there waiting for you? I mean, after all, this is one of the most awesome benefits of personal development and working with your intuition that I can think of!

Let's talk about how to connect intuitively every day in every way you possibly can. When you are really focusing on your intuitive

## 12. LIVE AS THE GURU IN YOU

work every day, your connections to Spirit will increase. You will begin to sense energy. As you do, you will begin to feel part of something much bigger than yourself. You may feel that there are times when *you are not alone*, even when you are physically the only person in the room. This is how you will know that you are developing a sense of the spirit realm.

Often in the beginning, this will happen during a dream so vivid you question whether it was *really* a dream. Or it could happen during a guided meditation. At some point you will feel, sense, or hear thoughts coming into your head and mind. You will think that it is just your imagination. It is not. You will think that you are just making it up. You are not. You will have to practice and learn to identify when it is your brain talking and when it is not. All these little intuitive nudges you are beginning to work with are your higher self, your Spirit Guides, and your Angels. Everybody has them. Everyone. Including you.

As you become practiced at attuning yourself to the subtle realms of energy, you will at some point detect a presence that seems to be outside yourself. Often there is confusion when beginning to connect with Guides because their communication with you can appear to come from inside your own mind. Know that there is a certain telepathy involved in most spirit communication. Therefore at times, thoughts and ideas can seem to be coming from your own mind even though you may sense an external presence around you. Guides and Angels use our soul's voice to communicate with us.

Through practice, you will begin to gain confidence in the information that you are sensing and receiving. In time, you will learn to know the difference between your own thoughts and those being communicated from Spirit. Your Guides and

Angels are there to help, assist, protect, and direct you. When you learn to develop and nurture your relationship with your Guides and Angels, you will be able to make use of their wonderful assistance.

There are some things to keep in mind when working with your Guides and Angels. Sometimes the relationship is a deeply intimate one, and sometimes it is not. You have different Guides and Angels for different purposes and at different times in your life. Sometimes the encounter is short and sometimes it will last a lifetime.

There is a hierarchy in the Spirit world and Spirit Guides are not usually Angels. For the most part Angels are of an exalted order and have their own hierarchy, though they can and will provide guidance and protection. Generally with Spirit Guides, the scope and focus of their work is not on the same scale and importance as Angels. Generally, our Spirit Guides tend to focus on the ordinary and mundane aspects of our day-to-day lives. They help us navigate daily life and assist us in learning our life lessons as we do so. They are our friends, helpers, companions, comforters, mentors, and teachers. Sometimes our deceased relatives and friends can act as Spirit Guides, but this is not always or even usually the case. That is not to say that our family members in spirit cannot have guiding moments or actions, they can, it is just not often that this is the focus of their work or how they spend their time. They are still learning and growing as individual souls and are still on their own soul journey's.

The more you practice connecting to and working with your Spirit Guides and Angels and invite their participation into your life, the stronger your relationship with them will become. I know they are very excited to work with you! Creating balance and harmony in your life will increase your ability to connect

## 12. LIVE AS THE GURU IN YOU

with them. Keeping your vibration as highly aligned with your spiritual mind as possible is very important when you want to actively work with your Spirit Guides and Angels. Remember the Law, *like attracts like*.

You can begin to work actively with your Guides by practicing asking questions for specific knowledge and guidance. Most importantly, do not get hung up on details like who they are, what their age is, what their name is, what their gender or race, things like that. Worrying about those details is just your ego taking over and it can become a distraction and at worse, a block. Only two things matter when working with your Guides: the strength of your connection and the message they are giving you. Keep your focus on these two things.

If you do not meditate regularly yet, begin now with a daily practice. Even just fifteen minutes a day will make a real difference. Daily meditation is the single most important step in connecting with Spirit. It is the best way to get to know yourself and tap into your Divine power, as well as cultivating your intuition.

Always remain open and flexible to how information presents itself to you. We are all wired uniquely, and you must learn how it is that you connect to, feel, and communicate with Spirit. This process is as unique to you as your fingerprints are. Once you figure out how you connect with Spirit and the more you practice doing it, the more regular the communication will become. Do your best to stay in your creative brain and leave the assessing and analyzing until after your connection session or meditation. Simply let yourself experience, perceive, and receive without expectation or thinking.

As I mentioned, I began meditating when I was 17 years old. There have been times when it was a major focus of my life and others when it was not. Always however, there has been maintenance. For me, it becomes very obvious when I have fallen off the wagon of my meditation practice. Whenever I become frustrated or short tempered, experience brain fog, or even feel down, I know that it is time to reboot my meditation practice. Life gets on top of all of us, that is only natural. What matters is that you have the tools you need to get you back on track.

Even though my meditation practice has ebbed and flowed over the years each day I make it a point to connect with God, the Universe, and my Guides and Angels. To be honest, I am not sure I know what it is like to be disconnected. Honouring all of that in my life and voicing my gratitude for it all is for me like brushing my teeth, it's just part of my routine. I suppose I could refer to it as my spiritual hygiene. I just do not feel right in myself if I do not take the time to connect. Sometimes this takes on a formal practice and other times it is merely an internal conversation that I have with Spirit. Each day I say, "Hello Angels, hello everyone, thank you so much for being in my life." Then usually I take a few minutes to tune into everything and get a sense of what I need to do for the day. I tune into my body to see what it needs. I ask for guidance to help me navigate the day and I ask to be guided to what God needs me to do that day.

For me, it is that simple. It can be as little as a 10-minute conversation in my mind with the Universe, or it can be include a formal meditation practice, or sitting in a channeling session with my Guides. The only rule I have is to honour my connection to God and the Universe and reaffirm my commitment to working as an instrument of both. The rest I leave up to those higher powers. I trust and know that I will be told what to do, how to do it, and that I will be taken care of along the way. This is how I live as the guru in me.

## The Rest Of The Story

Speaking to a publisher about my book with such ease and confidence was surreal. The interview with her about my book idea went well, and we had a great chat about all things spiritual. I discussed myself, my life, and my book concept. I was reassured by her relaxed and professional manner and she seemed exactly as she was on her YouTube videos, which was really refreshing. I was feeling truly blessed to have met her in this way, inspired and encouraged. We wrapped up the session and she told me that they would be making the final decision within a week about which authors would be chosen to be published as part of the contest. She said that she would let me know either way by email, and that was that.

Over the next week, I tried not to think about it all. In one of her following YouTube videos, she announced again a last call out to spiritual authors and it unfolded that they had bumped the final number up to seven from four because the talent was so awesome, that it had become impossible to narrow things down. This gave me a bit of a sinking feeling in the pit of my stomach, testing my confidence. However, before too long, I got my thinking around to being happy whatever the outcome was to be. I also prepared myself to wait longer than a week to find out.

True to her word, a week later I received an email in my inbox as promised. I had thought that I was nervous the last time, but now I was feeling a bit over the top. I just dove right in. To my utter shock, delight, amazement, and immense pleasure, I read that I had indeed been chosen! I was informed that once the final people had been notified, a group call with her and the publisher and the other selected people would be organized. I was informed that for the next 10 months we would be mentored by her personally, and then we were to be handed off to the publisher. I could not believe my luck! I was inwardly beyond excited. I felt like so many pieces of my life puzzle were finally snapping into place. I vowed to myself that I would make the absolute most of this opportunity, and I believe I have.

The synchronicities in life are truly a wonder. About six years ago I had a client come to me for a reading. During her session, I had an uncanny feeling that I was going to become friends with her and what is more, I felt I would work with her in some way, it was most curious. It turned out that she was a professional editor and her specialization was the very genre that I would write about. She had more than 20 years experience and knew the publishing world inside and out. She was also a ghost writer and had written many books for psychics and sensitives. She was also one of the nicest and most authentic people I had ever met. We clicked right away, and I knew exactly who I would go to for help with editing my work. Snap.

The past year has been a bit of a whirlwind and if I am honest, at times I have felt overwhelmed with it all. It has been a *huge* struggle balancing my new commitments with my existing ones. I have learned a lot, that is for sure. I know I still I have a lot to learn, and I am OK with this because I know and trust the workings of the Universe and its process. I know firsthand that being able to put your fears aside and take inspired action will work out in your favour every time.

Regardless of a specific result, taking action re-establishes your energetic position within yourself and with the Universe. When you act, you are telling the Universe that you are committed to co-creating and that you are open and willing to do your part. That is all that is necessary to garner support and energy in return. If you do this continuously in your life, listening to your

## 12. LIVE AS THE GURU IN YOU

intuition along the way and marrying that with action, your life will upshift and open in amazing ways you never imagined. The Universe does support you, and what's more, it wants you to succeed in marvelous ways. I am living proof of this. My life is living proof that this works, and I urge you to live as the Guru in you.

Remember we are all works in progress and everything is a process. Prioritizing your life to cultivate success is necessary to assist you in your intuitive development. The most important thing when working intuitively is to come from a place of balance (physically, emotionally, mentally, and spiritually) and neutrality, both as you work and as you discern the information that you receive.

Who you are and how you work and interact with the world around you will change as you grow personally and intuitively. Your process is unique to you, and therefore please know that there is no right and wrong way to do things. Just settle in to how you work and trust your journey. Ask for help along the way when you need it. As your energy awareness accelerates, you will begin to sense a connection to something bigger than yourself. In time you will begin to sense a connection to the Spirit world. Your *sensing* can be from hearing, seeing, feeling, smelling, thought, and more. Sensing can take on many forms and even become a mixture of these. It is all about you and your process.

# Intuitive Training Tip#13 – Connecting with Your Sprit Guides

Here is an exercise for you to try. Practice it again and again until it becomes second-nature for you to connect regularly with your Guides and Angels. Read through it first before you try it so that you get the gist of what to do.

From your mind or with your voice, outwardly tell your Guides you wish to have a meeting with them. You can call it a *connection session*. You can make this request to them in advance or just before the session, either way it will set the intention and tell your Guides that you want to connect.

Here are some great questions to go through each time you practice connecting to your Guides. Read through them all before your meditation and familiarize yourself with the content ideas. After your *connection session*, go through them all and try to write down what you remember. The practice of this technique will help you build a rapport with your Guides and assist you in establishing a process that works for you. The question topics over time will become embedded in your mind as a sort of protocol to follow each time you try to connect or schedule an official connection session. Once you are having success and feeling confident in your process, then you can expand your conversations. Eventually the communication with your Guides will take on its own natural rhythm.

Prior to the meeting time, get yourself in a quieted state, relaxed and balanced with a neutral mind. You may want to meditate prior to your session. Whatever way you choose do it, enter a meditative, composed, and energetically-balanced state. Become as receptive as you possibly can. At the appointed time, in your *mind's-eye*, show up for the meeting.

## 12. LIVE AS THE GURU IN YOU

Be receptive. Sense anything in any way that comes to you and make a mental note of it.

Remember that sometimes Spirit uses telepathy to communicate to us. You may be hearing yourself talk to yourself in your mind or you may get a hunch or a physical feeling or flutter. Be open to whatever comes. Trust the information that you receive and tell yourself you will think about it all after the meeting.

If you feel that nothing happens, or that you did not sense anything, please do not get discouraged. Keep practicing. Your body and mind will eventually get used to this process and you will be able to relax into a more receptive state. Once you settle into this routine, things will change. Keep at it, and ask your Guides and Angels for help and for a sign that you are on the right track. Just keep open and relaxed, go through all the questions before hand, and see what comes. This may feel strange at first, but you can do this!

Describe all that you felt and sensed in your connection session.

_____
_____
_____
_____
_____
_____
_____

Did you feel a connection directly with a Guide (a source of information that you sensed came from Spirit versus from your intellectual mind)?

_____
_____
_____
_____
_____
_____
_____

How did this Guide (or connection) help you today?

_____
_____
_____
_____
_____
_____
_____

Did you perceive any new ideas or information about yourself and where you are at in your life right now?

_____
_____
_____
_____
_____
_____
_____

## 12. LIVE AS THE GURU IN YOU

How did you perceive or receive your information? How did you feel in your body during the session?

_____
_____
_____
_____
_____
_____
_____

Did you notice or sense anything specific about the place or space where you first sensed your connection?

_____
_____
_____
_____
_____
_____
_____

Did you have a sense of knowing what the purpose of your connection was?

_____
_____
_____
_____
_____
_____
_____

Did this source or Guide feel familiar to you in any way?

_____
_____
_____
_____
_____
_____
_____

Were there any specific messages relayed to you?

_____
_____
_____
_____
_____
_____
_____

Do you feel that you want to connect with this guiding energy again?

_____
_____
_____
_____
_____
_____
_____

## 12. LIVE AS THE GURU IN YOU

Again, if on this occasion if you did not sense any specific energy that in any way you felt could be guidance from a source outside yourself, keep at it. Try again and again. Try meditation with some of these questions in mind and ask Spirit (out loud) for assistance in connecting you with your Spirit Guides. With practice, it will come to you.

## **Quick Recap:**

Every one of us has Spirit Guides and Angels. Whether you have experienced connecting with them or not, they are here with you right now. Through the practice of meditation and trying to connect to Spirit, you will eventually sense your Spirit Guides and Angels. Remember when you are working intuitively, and actively trying to connect, you will serve yourself best by getting into a receptive meditative state. Achieve a neutral mind and be sure you are centered and grounded.

Often our Guides use spiritual telepathy to communicate with us, and what you sense may present in the form of your own thoughts, ideas, or visions. You may feel, envision, hear thoughts, or have images come to your mind. Remember that this is a creative process, and that your imagination works in conjunction with Spirit. Your intuitive thoughts become a tool for their communication.

The trial and error of practice are ultimately what will develop your confidence and your trust in working intuitively, and indeed your skill. Enjoy your intuitive journey as you Awaken the Guru in You.

# RECOMMENDED FOR YOU

This is a list of books that have helped me on my intuitive and life journey.

- *You Can Heal Your Life* by Louise Hay

- *Eastern Body Western Mind* by Anodea Judith

- *Frontiers of Health* by Christine R. Page

- *Creative Visualization* by Shakti Gawain

- *Increase Your Energy – Regain Your Zest for Life the Natural Way* by Louis Proto

- *The Eagle and the Rose* by Rosemary Altea

- *River of Life How to Live in the Flow* by Marilyn. J. Awtry

- *Mediumship Explained* by E.W and M.H. Wallis

- *Becoming a Practical Mystic* by Jacqueline Small

- *Turning the Mind into an Ally* by Sakyong Mipham

# ABOUT THE AUTHOR

Trish Ottone has been working as a psychic-medium and intuitive advisor for more than 25 years helping people develop their intuition and deepening their understanding of energy and the psycho-spiritual components of their lives. She believes that everyone is intuitive and that we all have the ability to connect to that place deep within where our own innate wisdom resides.

Trish studied politics in university and completed a formal diploma in advertising, which opened the door to her first career which spanned 10 successful years in corporate marketing. Then following her own inner calling, she left that behind to create a holistic career as an intuitive and healer. Over the years, Trish has achieved professional credentials in Holisitic Nutrition, Clinical Hypnotherapy, as well as others, and she is a Certified Life Coach. She has also spent many years teaching Hatha yoga and meditation.

Trish works out of her Victorian home near Stratford, Ontario, Canada where she lives with her family happily continuing her client work, writing books, and enjoying her garden.

www.trishottone.com

Instagram: @trishottone

www.ingramcontent.com/pod-product-compliance
Lightning Source LLC
Chambersburg PA
CBHW071608080526
44588CB00010B/1058